DREADFUL SORRY

DREADFUL SORRY

ESSAYS ON AN AMERICAN NOSTALGIA

JENNIFER NIESSLEIN

Belt Publishing

Printed in the United States of America
First edition 2022
1 2 3 4 5 6 7 8 9

ISBN: 978-1-953368-03-4

Belt Publishing
5322 Fleet Avenue
Cleveland, Ohio 44105
www.beltpublishing.com

Cover art by David Wilson
Book design by Meredith Pangrace

For my family

TABLE OF CONTENTS

INTRODUCTION

In the summer of 2019, my three sisters and I, along with our families and our father, converged on Deep Creek Lake in western Maryland. We've been coming here since we were girls; our paternal great-grandfather had once owned a cottage on this lake. On this trip, Dad went fishing with my husband early one morning and pointed out which cottage it was.

I didn't know Grandpap Yukevich well, but I met him at least once. I remember a tall man in his seventies with a booming voice. In 1957, he and his second wife, Vivian, endured a home invasion when a relative by marriage broke into their home above his car dealership, beat them, and stole $41,000 they'd stored in a safe. Less than a month later, it happened again. The antibiotics Grandpap Yukevich, was given for his injuries left him deaf, so when I met him I wrote notes to communicate. He died in 1979, so I couldn't have been older than seven. I have fuzzy memories of staying at the cabin, none of them from a higher perspective than a kitchen countertop.

The cottage itself hasn't been in the family—or at least acknowledged family—for decades. After Grandpap Yukevich died, Vivian was the sole inheritor of his estate. When she died in a nursing home four years later, the story goes, the cottage became part of her estate and she left it to a nephew. This nephew is rumored to actually be Vivian and Grandpap Yukevich's son, conceived and born when Grandpap was still married to my great-grandmother. It's just a rumor, but my great-grandfather was allegedly sketchy enough in his younger days that we descendants believe it.

Anyway, as we left town, my husband, son, and I went to check out the cottage. We drove slowly down the street until we spotted the white picket fence my great-grandfather had installed. Someone had built an addition, adding two more bedrooms and an extra bathroom. I spotted a rental sign at the top of the driveway with a website to visit if you wanted to stay at "Lakeside Fun," as the new owner dubbed it.

I felt a strange yearning for that cottage. Maybe it's because so much of my family history is a study in poverty and deprivation, and this represented something of enduring value (somewhere between $500,000 and $600,000, I'd find later) while many of my ancestors were seen as disposable people during their lifetimes. Maybe it was a pride thing, showing off that I could afford a lost piece of the family holdings, if only for a week. I suspect, though, that my main motivation came from someplace more primal: the cottage represented a crumb of my idyllic childhood. The world itself has always been complicated, and for many, if not most of, its inhabitants, unfair and brutal. But my childhood world—a relatively sheltered existence, catching lightning bugs with my sisters and eating Mom's pot roast and hosing off lake bottom muck from my feet—was simple and sweet.

Four hours later, we were back home in Charlottesville, and I was already on the computer. The property next door to Lakeside Fun—"Sunny Escape"— was also a rental, and together, the two houses were big enough to fit the whole crew.

My sisters and I booked them by the end of the week.

———————

I have a nostalgia problem, and I'm not the only American who does.

Not long ago, a friend and local journalist shared on Facebook the news that a Confederate statue outside the Albemarle County courthouse (located in the city) would come down. One of her friends commented that he understood why it had to be removed, but he had such good memories of playing as a child near it in the parklike setting as he waited for his uncle, a judge, to get off work.

I couldn't relate to his memory in any factual sense. I didn't grow up with Confederate monuments, and even knowing a judge outside the courtroom would have been beyond my family's reach, but I recognized and respected the wistfulness of his remark.

It's not always so benign. In September, a state circuit court judge denied a group of die-hard white southerners the $500 each they sought for emotional damage they suffered when the city shrouded two Confederate monuments in tarps for 188 days. However, the judge awarded the group attorney and litigation fees. The seven plaintiffs are asking in excess of $600,000, and the case is still tied up in legal knots.

I am literally going to pay for someone else's nostalgia.

———————

The idea of nostalgia predates the United States itself. In her acclaimed 2001 book, *The Future of Nostalgia*, the late Svetlana Boym traced the term back to the Swiss doctor Johannes Hofer, who coined it in 1688. For this new medical diagnosis, he drew from his observations of "various displaced people of the seventeenth century, freedom-loving students from the Republic of Berne studying in Basel, domestic help and servants working in France and Germany and Swiss soldiers fighting abroad." They all displayed, basically, homesickness for where they came from.

To boil down Boym's complex and fascinating work, nostalgia then, for the most part, was seen as a primarily European and Russian fascination. It moved from a medical issue (back when doctors theorized about some mysterious body part that might be the key) to one left to philosophy and the arts. Nostalgia was first considered a disease to be cured, then an unsavory character trait to be snuffed out. It's been in and out of fashion: the European Romantics embraced nostalgia, while the Industrial Revolution era found nostalgics unsophisticated people, their necks craned away from the promise of the future.

Our modern understanding of nostalgia has evolved. Now, nostalgia isn't just a simple longing for a homeland —it's a longing for a lost time. Whether it's a yen for a time in your beloved childhood home or for your favorite decade, it's impossible to actually revisit. "Nostalgia is a rebellion against the modern idea of time, the time of history and progress," Boym maintains.

When the United States was shiny and new, it had no use for Europe's nostalgia. The founders billed the nation as one in which people could break free from that musty European rule. Boym cites American doctors who claimed our country's citizens didn't even have nostalgia. At least, that is, until the Civil War. Theodore Calhoun, a Union military doctor, found it in his soldiers, Boym wrote. He thought of nostalgia as a weakness, something fairly girly. "In boarding school, as perhaps many of us will remember, ridicule is wholly relied upon. … [The nostalgic] patient can often be laughed out of it by his comrades, or reasoned out of it by appeals to his manhood," Calhoun asserted. (Is there *anything* toxic masculinity can't solve?)

The United States has aged, and the old gray mare ain't what she used to be. Many of us—and many of our institutions—cling to nostalgia, and in fact have built both personal identities and cultural identities on it.

I'm an American nostalgic, with all the symptoms diagnosed back in the European and Russian olden days. I look back at my younger days in a golden light, putting aside what history shows was going on at the time. I come from a background of displacement, albeit less traumatic than writers who've been, for ethnic and political reasons, forced from their homelands. I'm an American northerner who has lived in the South most of my life, a girl with working-class roots who grew up to be a relatively affluent woman, the most educated of my sisters, but who is still somehow both the least practically skilled *and* one of the least educated people in my neighborhood.

Nostalgia appeals to me because it can link us to the past—a kind of gateway to understanding our history. As an armchair genealogist, I started off with my Ancestry.com account, earnestly looking to verify the family stories I'd heard. I yearned to get as close as I could to understanding the family patterns and their origins—the stuff that shapes who we become. As Michael Chabon wrote in "The True Meaning of Nostalgia" in a 2017 issue of the *New Yorker*, "Nostalgia, most truly and most meaningfully, is the emotional experience—always momentary, always fragile—of having what you lost or never had, of seeing what you missed seeing, of meeting the people you missed knowing, of sipping coffee in the storied cafés that are now hot-yoga studios." (My people were sipping something a bit stronger than coffee, but I pick up what he's putting down.)

And even Boym maintains nostalgia can have its benefits, primarily by uniting us. I couldn't have written this book without consulting my sisters, especially Erin, just twenty-three months younger than me. We've always been close. For some of our childhood years, maybe a little too close for my liking—Erin didn't just read my diary; the girl *wrote* in it. But our shared memories and the memories we've created now have only made us closer. I love my membership in this Niesslein sisters-and-mom unit the same way I love my place in my own small family, the way all of us bond through shared experience. It gives me a safe harbor, people who can confirm that, hey, I'm not nuts—this is how life really happened, no matter what the cultural narrative says.

But by definition, nostalgia is regressive, backward-looking. Both personally and societally, nostalgia challenges the validity of memories of those who recall events differently. On a personal level, it's bad enough: one family member remembers a time of strife while another recalls that period as idyllic; some classmates return to a twenty-year reunion to revisit the good old days while others think of those four years as hell, or at least a sort of purgatory.

In severe cases, personal nostalgia can be bad even for the person having it. It's entirely possible to rut yourself so completely out of time that you cannot have a genuine moment in the present. As André Aciman writes in *False*

Papers in an essay on Marcel Proust, "How could Marcel have ever loved such a place? Or had he never loved it? Had he loved only the act of returning to it on paper, because that was how he lived his life—first by wanting to live it, and later remembering having wanted to, and ultimately by writing about the two? The part in between—the actual living—was what had been lost." I'm not that far gone, most of the time. If anything, my childhood displacement makes me more like a plant than a rolling stone: plop me down somewhere and I'll try to grow roots no matter how fertile the soil.

Nostalgia has the ability to unite us on a wider scale, too—but it can also be outright dangerous, depending on what we unite for. As a culture, we've romanticized revolutionary figures in American history so much that it's become the job of writers and historians to remind the public exactly how how revolutionary—and dangerous— they were considered in the times they lived in. It took real bravery to be Martin Luther King Jr. or Nellie Bly. The very existence of Confederate battle flags and Columbus Day speak to how nostalgia leads to the denial of historical fact. I live in Charlottesville, Virginia, and I've seen firsthand what happens when white men romanticize the past, whether it's the Confederacy, the Nazi regime, or some fuzzy idea that the natural order is white men first. In times of backlash against progress, both the regressive powerful and the regressive fringe look to the past. For most of us, the very worst of it.

———————

This is a collection about American nostalgia—specifically my American nostalgia. My life experience won't transport you around the world or even around the country. You can pretty much start driving in the morning at one point in my lifetime migration, stop for a nice lunch and a few breaks, and still get to your destination before the sun sets. My American nostalgia is a dive through time. I've always been more interested in ordinary people than historical figures. I don't give a hoot about military strategies—just tell me what people in the olden days used for toilet paper. I'm writing this as an ordinary person who came from other ordinary people. I hope this book sparks something in you about your own ordinary history.

———————

In March 2020, the global COVID-19 pandemic hit the United States, and my sisters and I cancelled our June trip to Lakeside Fun and Sunny Escape. I'd planned on writing about it for this collection. Would the apple tree—where Mom picked fruit to makes apple pies—still be there? Would the kitchen I vaguely remember still exist? Would the walls still hold the faint scent of my ancestors' cigarettes?

It's still a mystery. There's always more nostalgia in the future.

BEFORE WE WERE
GOOD WHITE

"That's where they found her body."

I nose the rented minivan onto the side of the narrow road, and Gram and I get out. It's a lovely little grassy patch that slopes down to a sun-dappled creek. Or *crick*, as we call it.

"She had one arm raised above her head," Gram says, "like someone dragged her there."

When I think of western Pennsylvania fondly, it's summer that I'm remembering: the greens of the trees and grass, the bursts of neon yellow from lightning bugs, the red tomatoes from the garden up on the windowsill. But Pennsylvania in the winter is, frankly, depressing—the grim black-and-white tableau—with the black mountains, the stark white snow, the clumps of gray frozen along the turnpike. It's a place where the coal mines have made their mark, and slate piles still stand.

When she died on January 22, 1932, it was cold and the forecast had called for rain. It's likely her body was found soaked, her long skirts muddied and maybe bloodied. I imagine the creek's waters rising toward that arm.

She's my Gram's grandmother, my great-great-grandmother. Growing up, I only knew three things about her: The legend was that her husband, a coal-miner like so many Polish immigrants, was in "frail health," and as a result, she took up bootlegging—and was successful enough at it to own three houses. Her fourth child, her youngest, was rumored to be of mixed race. And she was murdered.

How could I resist mythologizing her? On these barest of bones, I pressed on flesh that reflected the fantasy of who I'd be if my back were to the wall. A badass! A proto-feminist! An outlaw! A woman who landed on her feet when times got tough! Myths, of course, always represent the imagination of the mythmaker. I didn't even know her first name or what she looked like, but I was eager to find a woman in my lineage who didn't play by the rules.

Mom told me that Gram didn't like to talk about her, so when I was a kid, I didn't dare broach the subject. She was a warm grandmother and doted on us, asking my sisters and me to sing songs on their breezy porch, teaching us Scrabble and Boggle, and rewarding us with small gifts. But there were unspoken rules to be followed, enforced by the time-honored code of passive aggression. We—especially as girls—were to appear "neat" (a massive compliment in Gram's eyes), not bicker, attend church regularly, and excel in school. Gram didn't smoke or drink or swear. The most outrageous thing she did on a regular basis was to wiggle out of her bra while driving, twirl it on her index finger, then fling it onto the back seat of her Cadillac.

Sometime in my twenties, Gram and I became friends. She'd loosened up by then; she'd occasionally have a glass of pink wine when her son-in-law encouraged her, and she let my boyfriend and me sleep in the same bed when we visited. When I became a mother, we grew closer, swapping tales of motherhood, then and now. (If only for the accessibility of washing machines, now is better.) In recalling the hard times, Gram reverts to the second person.

In my thirties, I felt close enough to Gram to ask directly about her grandmother. What happened? We talked, and over the course of several years, I pieced together the memories and legends with possibly the only person alive who actually knew her.

I told Gram I'd do some research. "Be careful," she

warned me. "There are some people in the family you don't want to talk to."

This was code. Not every relative had become respectable.

———————

When someone is a myth, it's easy to forget that she was also a person.

Her name was Anna Dec Fisher. She and my great-great-grandfather John emigrated from Poland. Her first name was sometimes "Annie," and their last name wasn't really Fisher. According to census records, their true last name might have been Ezoeske, Jezorski, or Yozarski. They spoke Polish, and a few fragments of their language still run in my family. "*Zamknij się*" means "Shut your mouth." "*Jest zimno*" means "It's cold." We, the descendants, have bastardized the foreign phrases to accommodate our American tongues.

Annie and John immigrated in 1901, a time when the United States was still figuring out how to sort the new waves of immigrants into the racial categories it had constructed. Poles were technically white, placing them above some races, but not the right kind of white. Or maybe the right kind for certain interests. Bluntly put,

Poles were considered by WASP America as strong and hardworking—the perfect fit for manual labor—but stupid. Ralph Waldo Emerson, approvingly, wrote in 1852, "Our idea, certainly, of Poles and Hungarians is little better than of horses recently humanized." (Oh, Ralphie, go shoot your eye out.) A US Steel Corporation want ad from 1909 read, in part, "Syrians, Poles, and Romanians preferred."

Annie wasn't stupid. She was just new. It's unclear if she and John landed in the US together, but they came from different parts of what was Poland, which didn't technically exist as a country in 1901. John was from Galacia, the poorest region of Europe at the time, then in Austrian Poland. Annie claimed Russian Poland. They started off their new lives together in Ohio, where their first child, Mary, was born, followed by Helen (my great-grandmother, Gram's mom) and Walter. By 1910, they were in Walkertown, a small town in West Pike Run Township, Pennsylvania. John worked as a coal miner. It's where their last child, Adam, would be born.

The first photo I saw of Annie was one that my distant cousin Nicole shared with me. It's a family photo from before Adam was born. Annie is standing, one hand on her hip, the other holding Helen's hand. Her hair's styled in one of those froufy buns popular around the turn of the century. She wears a bow tie on her puffy white shirt, and a full-length skirt.

By the April 1920 census, they already owned their own home, free of a mortgage. In January that year, the government had enacted the eighteenth amendment, also known as Prohibition. At some point, Annie and John started breaking the new law.

I started finding more artifacts, and the myth of Annie started breaking down. A different picture of her emerged from the bath of historical documents and the context of her life. And that picture of Annie's life and how she spent it would haunt my family all the way down to my own upraising.

"My dad said everyone did it," Mom told me, referring to the Prohibition-era law.

"Yes," I said. "But not everyone went to jail for it."

———————

Walkertown was small, and people talked. Adam was born in 1916 and was not yet five at the time of the 1920 census. The census taker seemed to be confused. In the column for race, an "Mu" for "mulatto" is marked, then written over more strongly with a "W" for "white."

It wasn't just the census taker. There seemed to have been a nongovernmental consensus as well that John wasn't Adam's father. Gram told me that when she was a kid, sometimes she'd go to the movie theater where Adam worked. He'd let her in for free. But neither would get too close because, you know, the rumors. Later, Adam would leave Walkertown, marry a white redhead, and join the military. Outside of Walkertown, as far as I know, no one questioned his whiteness.

Nicole is also the one who first showed me pictures of Adam. He was a handsome guy, although slightly darker than the other Fisher siblings. This doesn't mean a lot to me; I have an uncle with a darker skin tone than his siblings, too. Genes pop up in the most peculiar ways.

This interracial brouhaha is so unremarkable now that I feel ridiculous bringing it up, but then I remember that sometimes my grandparents would explain their youths to me in ways that could only be seen as racist: *Dating an Italian was almost as bad as dating a Black.* Meaning, in the poor white community, you lost status. You lost your advantage, which was the measure of respect that your skin color afforded you. The only thing that kept you from being at the very bottom of the American pecking order. Even the *rumor* of blackness was enough to awaken the racism of Walkertown.

I wonder sometimes if the people of Walkertown would have even questioned Adam's race had there not been a man, labeled by the census as "mulatto," living next door to Annie and John. Short of finding Adam's descendants and convincing them to give me a quarter teaspoonful of their spit to send to an online DNA profiler, I'm not going to know. I don't need to know; we're judged on how we present, not on who we are, anyway. Annie could well have had an affair with the guy next door. But she just as easily—more easily, actually—could have been friendly to her next-door neighbor. Or, easier still, she could have done nothing at all.

All the rumors mean is that Annie was the kind of woman who her white peers thought capable of crossing the line between proper and improper. Whether Adam was John's son or not, they were right. Annie was a woman who crossed lines.

———

By the summer of 1929, if Annie hadn't earned respect through piety and birthright, she was grabbing it in the real American way: with money.

Two of Annie's children had married and had had children of their own. According to the family, Annie owned three houses by then. Her oldest, Mary, lived with her family in one. Helen lived with her family in the multiunit house next to Annie, John, Walter, and Adam.

Annie was bootlegging. She was good at it. I believe she was the brains of the couple, able to read and write while John couldn't. Gram remembers the yard filled with cars. She was young, just five when her grandmother died, too young to understand that these were probably the cars of paying customers visiting her grandparents.

On July 29, 1929, police raided Annie and John's house. According to police reports, Helen yelled, "Beat it! The law is coming!"

I imagine customers scrambled into those parked cars and beat it with a quickness.

Next, Helen dumped out a pitcher of liquor that was on the back porch and told the cops, "Go ahead and search. The evidence is gone."

The evidence wasn't gone. They found sixteen quarts of beer, two barrels of wine, and a quarter gallon of moonshine in a gallon jug.

Annie, John, and Helen were arrested.

———

I questioned the documents that I received from Washington County. Did the woman I knew as Grandma

Crawford, the permed lady with the puffy pink toilet seat and yappy dog named Duchess, really call out, "Beat it!"?

But then I remember how notoriously blunt and mouthy she was. When I was a kid, she accused me of cheating at 500 Rum and made me cry. When her daughter-in-law and her son-in-law left her children for each other, her remark was, "Why would he leave one fat one"—her daughter—"for another fat one?" When my parents separated, she cut to the chase—no *I'm sorry, honey*—and offered Mom money if she could live with us. (We didn't have anywhere to put her.)

And looking at photos of her when she was a teenager, with her bobbed hair and defiant face, I could believe it.

But I also believe that the arrest changed something in Helen.

The next morning, John was charged with manufacturing and possession. Annie and Helen were charged with sale and possession. The bail was $1,000 for Annie, and $500 each for John and Helen. None of them could make bail, so they sat in the Washington County jail.

They sat there for a while.

This was news to Gram. When I told her, she immediately asked, "Where was I?"

She would have been not quite three years old when

the arrest happened. My breath caught, realizing that this isn't some historical curiosity, that I can't stand on my middle-class perch and think that my research doesn't have real-life ramifications, just as modern-day journalism doesn't have ramifications for its subjects, especially ones whose names show up in the crime blotter, not the society pages, of the newspaper. My voice softened. "Your dad's mom, Amanda, lived with you then, Gram. I bet she took good care of you."

On August 21, 1929, the testimonies of the law enforcement officers were entered into the record. On September 9, 1929, John, Annie, and Helen went before a judge. John and Annie pled guilty at some point—perhaps that day—but Helen did not. On October 1, 1929, the district attorney filed a motion with the court for a *nolle prosequi* (meaning that the state acknowledges it doesn't have enough evidence against the defendant to prosecute) for Helen. He noted that Helen's parents were now serving their sentences. I don't know what those sentences were, but they've become irrelevant in the story of my family. I spoke to a friend with a legal degree, and she suspected that Annie and John's plea deal included the stipulation that Helen would go home. She'd already been in jail for over two months.

Helen had missed Gram's third birthday during her time there; her son was five years old, her second daughter just an infant. Her breasts must have ached terribly, lumpy and swollen with milk. I think of her there, now a twenty-three-year-old married mother, in an iron and steel facility once called "a modern-day Bastille." I can't imagine the shame that must have plagued her, the dignity robbed. I can imagine, though, that the experience strengthened her already-entrenched resolve to, above all else, become respectable.

I was well into adulthood before I heard of respectability politics, and I only learned of them in the context of Black history. In a nutshell, it means when a group outside of the mainstream tries to assimilate in order to become accepted. The opposite is when a group outside the mainstream refuses to prove their own exceptionalism or even acceptability to the dominant group. (I cribbed the terms "exceptional" and "acceptable" from Traci D. O'Neal's powerful 2018 book, *The Exceptional Negro: Racism, White Privilege, and the Lie of Respectability Politics.*) In terms of race, only white people have historically been able to win the respectability game because we don't carry any visible markers that we're "different." We can dress like the respected class; we can adopt their mannerisms, their biases, their way of speaking.

We can, but not all of us do. The people who don't are the people Gram spoke of, the ones I shouldn't want to know, like the relatives who came to my grandfather's viewing and were caught rifling through the pockets of the mourners' coats. As now-respectable white people, we don't know what to do with them, even as we know their personal histories and how much they would have had to overcome to have a shot at mainstream lives. They're not the rebels we mythologize. They're problems to be avoided because they've proven they will fuck us over in real time.

I see our family's striving for respectability in an artifact. There's a photo of John and two friends, the Novak brothers, in my grandmother's box of old photos. (I've changed the family's last name out of respect for their descendants.) Written on the photo is "The Drunks." I recognize the handwriting. I've seen it once a year for half of my life on birthday cards that arrived with a five-dollar bill tucked inside, signed, "Love, Great Grandma Crawford."

———————

Actually, I don't know for sure if the Novaks were Annie and John's friends. They seemed to have been, although God knows I've taken drunken photos with people who were little more than acquaintances.

In the year Annie would turn fifty-two years old, though, she went over to help Pete and Agnes Novak render lard from a recently slaughtered pig. One version of the story has her doing it out of the goodness of her heart and maybe for some portion of the lard. Another version has her working as hired help. In any case, by that time, John wasn't working; his lungs were severely compromised due to his time in the mines.

Annie didn't come home the night of January 22, 1932. Her body was found by the creek the next morning.

———————

I came to the story of Annie originally believing that I could Nancy Drew this sucker open and find out what really happened. Was she murdered? Was it some sort of cover-up? Were the Novaks ever implicated?

What I found out was that I'm so far removed from the underclass—by my own foremothers' design—that I took for granted that her suspicious death would warrant the kind of investigation that mine presumably would.

On January 25, 1932, Annie made the news in a noncriminal way for the first time. The *Charleroi Mail* (a newspaper from a town not far away) reported the headline, "Find Lifeless Body of Woman on Road; Heart Attack Victim":

> The lifeless body of Mrs. Anna Fisher, 52, of Walkertown, was discovered yesterday morning by John Hans, lying beside the road between Walkertown and Daisytown, near California [Pennsylvania].
>
> Deputy Coroner J.F. Timko, of California, stated that the woman had been dead about twelve hours when discovered. Mrs. Fisher had left the home of Pete [Novak] for her own home shortly after dark Friday evening. Members of her family were not alarmed over her absence because her husband was away from home. Death was due to a heart attack.
>
> She leaves her husband John Fisher, and four children: Walker and Andrew Fisher, at home, and Mrs. Helen Crawford and Mrs. Mary Smolley, both of Walkertown.

This wasn't journalism's finest moment. They got the date wrong, the spot wrong, and Walter's and Adam's names wrong. They probably even got her cause of death wrong.

Her death certificate lists her cause of death as "acute gastritis and enteritis" and states her death occurred around eleven at night.

Believing that the Novaks were her friends, I formed a story in my head in which Annie, who was likely a pretty hearty drinker, went to help the Novaks with the pig. While she was there, she died of natural causes. The Novaks—who didn't have such a clean record with law enforcement themselves, both with arrest records on alcohol-related charges—panicked and put her body by the creek.

I messaged Nicole about it, and she wasn't buying it.

"Did they do an autopsy?" she asked me.

I looked at the paper in front of me. "It's blank. So I guess not."

"Then how do they know?"

"Good point."

Later, with the help of a friend with medical knowledge, I looked into whether one can die of gastritis and enteritis. Turns out, people have actually died of it—

but the real cause of death is dehydration as a result of prolonged vomiting and diarrhea. It certainly doesn't seem like something that would cause you to keel over while walking home after rendering lard.

Nicole was right. We're never going to know.

When Gram and I visited, all of Annie's houses were still standing, although the movie theater wasn't there anymore and the general store was boarded up. Gram's knees were bothering her, but I held her hand—so much like mine, long-fingered and slim—and we made our way to Mary's former house, where a picture of Gram was taken so many years ago. That solemn, round face, those straight bangs and pageboy haircut. We knocked, but no one answered.

Annie's house was now painted a mustard yellow. Gram's childhood home was still white. As we stood there, a woman came out of one of its units. She didn't know any of the history, and besides, she was on her way to second shift.

After Annie died, the story goes that Mary didn't pay the taxes on the houses (why she was the one in charge, I have no idea), and they were taken by the government. Helen's family wound up in Daisytown, around the bend, in company housing.

We stopped there too, but we didn't get out. I have no poker face, and I think my expression showed the gulf between my life and hers. The houses were exactly as Gram had described them: one room that was the kitchen and everything else, two smaller rooms that served as bedrooms, no matter how many children your family had. The reality—the poverty—of it hadn't hit me until then. People still lived there. "That one was ours," Gram said, pointing. "At least we had an end one."

"I used to visit my grandfather when I was a kid," she said later. "We'd walk from Daisytown to Walkertown." I told her that the census reported that he didn't speak English, only Polish. She laughed. "He spoke English. I remember him as kind. He was gentle with us. He and Adam lived in a house that was half burned down, but he loved when we visited him."

When you're nostalgic for a time and place you've never experienced and a person you've never met, your nostalgia requires some imagination or at least some glossing over of the details. Driving back to my grandparents' house, I thought Gram had shielded me from the worst of her memories. Now, I'm not so sure she did. Maybe I'd imagined what she told me with that hazy, soft-focus lens of nostalgia. But seeing her childhood company housing in Daisytown clicked the lens away and transformed nostalgia into plain old history.

———————

With Annie transformed from a myth into a woman, I've had to face the myths that I built about myself.

When I was a kid, my family went though a rough patch, and it made a mark on me. Even before the steel industry imploded, we weren't financially stable, but once my dad got laid off, we were forced, for a time, to go on food stamps. I ate government cheese. We relocated to a different state and eventually gave our Pennsylvania home back to the bank. Those aren't the things that made the mark. It was the knowledge, even then, of the difference between someone's compassion for us and someone's pity—which is somehow worse than scorn. You can meet scorn with scorn; you can only meet pity with shame.

It's been more than three decades since I've been in that place, but I still think of myself as the underdog. I'm not. My own descendants—including my son, who (despite my fears) did not become an entitled little shit—will find that I'm a relatively rich woman, and any problems I've had with respectability are only visible if you know what to look for. My outlook embarrasses me; I lead a pretty damn charmed life and claiming otherwise is, I know, ridiculous. But I've clung to the underdog myth because part of me believes that I'd be incapable of showing compassion—not condescending pity, not scorn—to marginalized people if I hadn't, on some level, experienced it myself. I still grapple with the idea that compassion springs from who you are, not who you come from.

Try as I might, I can't let go of my own myth. Go ahead and search. The evidence isn't gone. It's just trace amounts at this point.

RESPECT

You know Aretha Franklin's "Respect"? The joy even in the opening chords? It's a great song, one of the best of the twentieth century.

I can't remember a time when I didn't know that Mom wanted it played at her funeral.

"Why can't you have hair like Nikki?" Gram would sigh, looking at Mom's friend.

Genetics would be the correct answer. Also accepted: Nikki's older sister was a hairdresser.

Mom had spent her life dealing with Gram's obsession with her thick, wavy hair. "I bet Ella wishes Nikki got the grades I did," she said. As soon as it came out of her mouth, she feared what hell Gram would raise. But this time, Gram didn't say anything.

Gram was, to put it mildly, a control freak. I believe it started with her quest for respectability, but eventually it became part of her personality. Even toward the end of her life, when blindness robbed her of the ability to cook, she'd taste food I'd made and tell me she'd have added an ingredient that no one's manufactured since 1982.

Back when Gram was a mother of underage kids, she couldn't control much. Not the disrespectable people with whom she shared both her maiden name and married name. Not the jobs accessible to her. Not even the day when she moved into the new home she and Pap built; she came home from work one day to find all of her stuff moved to the new place. (Gram and Pap called it "the foundation," but it was essentially an unfinished basement they partitioned off with thin boards; the idea was they'd build the top of it when they saved up the money. Mom was well into high school before that happened.)

Gram *could* control what went on in that home, though, and Mom and my aunt bore the brunt of that. Gram probably considered herself restrained, given the abuse she'd suffered as a kid, but she wasn't. She was exacting, with high expectations. Mom and my aunt took care of the house when Gram worked—there were two brothers, but the respectability rules didn't apply to them in the same way. Mom took charge of the cleaning and laundry. My aunt, four years her junior, was in charge of the cooking. By the time Gram came home, she expected the house to be spotless and their toddler brother to be bathed and clean.

The boys, on the other hand, had no housework to do. They were expected to mow the yard and shovel the driveway. Like a lot of places peopled by the poor, Mom's hometown put a lot of stock in sports—for years, a sports career could propel boys out of the mines (and later the mills and factories) into a life of comfort.

Girls had no such choices. "Girls only had a few career options growing up," Mom told me. "Teacher, nurse, hairdresser, or secretary." While she looked at her male extended family with embarrassment—drunken fistfights on Memorial Day in the graveyard, an Easter ham tossed out the window in a rage, police officers asking her the whereabouts of her rapist uncle in front of her friends— she took solace in the fact that her father's lineage included some schoolteacher aunts. "I knew early on that if I wanted a different life, I'd have to get there myself."

In the meantime, Mom lived with the rules: Respect your elders—although she knew there wasn't a thing respectable about many of the adults she knew, and found the rule confusing. Go to church—although her father didn't go after he found that the deacons greeted him as a brother on Sunday but ignored him on the job. Do well in school—although they had no resources at home to achieve it.

"We didn't have encyclopedias," Mom told me recently over the phone. She was making potato soup with what we call "gunchies." (Eggs, flour, and a touch of water mixed to the right consistency and dropped into a boiling liquid. It probably means something in my ancestors' Polish.)

"I had to go to either my Grandma Crawford's house or my Aunt Gloria's to read theirs." By the time Mom needed encyclopedias, a few of her relatives were nominally richer than her family. Their living room furniture wasn't lawn furniture, like hers was. "'Be sure to wash your hands,' is what they said. 'Don't get them dirty,'" Mom told me. "We were poor but I, of all people, know we weren't dirty. Mom wouldn't allow it.

"They made me feel less-than. It wasn't until I started making real money, after your father left, that I lost that feeling."

"That's horrible that your self-worth was tied to money," I said.

"Yes," she said. "It is."

She ordered our family a set of encyclopedias when I was a kid, although I'm sure they came with a payment plan. I can still feel the gilded-edge pages cracking when I opened them for the first time.

In my family, feminism has never been untethered from class.

When I was a kid, I'd only see flickers of the mean version of Gram. The first pictures of my sisters and me with our newborn sister Jill, show Erin and me with puffy eyes and red noses; Gram berated us for bickering over who got to hold the baby first. When my cousins were misbehaving at Gram's house, she asked if they wanted a whipping; with delight, they said yes, thinking a whipping would taste very good right about now. Gram also ruined my last day of high school by haranguing me about how my father had wronged my mother. She kept feigning a heart attack; I kept yelling back because Mom didn't raise me to fear anyone.

Over the years, Gram changed and mellowed. We became friends. The more financially successful her children became, the more comfortable she became with letting respectability politics fall away.

In one of my favorite pictures of Gram, she's in her eighties, sporting a black and pink wig. (We're a family that keeps wigs around for our own entertainment.) She's on the back of my sister's friend's motorcycle. She looks free.

My mother broke the cycle of respectability politics in our branch of the family. She didn't just want respectability. She wanted respect.

Mom was a feminist before it got a name. When she heard of the movement during her later years at a teachers' college, she thought it was just common sense. "I supported it. Of course we should get equal pay for equal work, and of course we should have the same rights as men," she tells me. "But I didn't march or anything." I've seen photos of her in college, all long legs with miniskirts and maxi-coats, a sheet of long wavy hair, her dazzling smile. She wasn't a hippie and she couldn't afford to blow her chance at a degree by getting arrested for anything—Mom's style was always changing the world person by person. Like Aretha says, she TCB. She's her own revolution.

I was born two years after Mom graduated from college. It would be magical thinking to believe her feminism was knit into my bones, infused in my cerebral fluid. But, unlike her, I grew up with her belief that I was smart *and* beautiful, kind *and* fierce. I have friends with lesser mothers; I wish they had Mom in their lives. There are only two rules: you must respect her and you cannot think you're cute.

———————

When I was growing up in the seventies and eighties, it was still the time of dumb blonde jokes, and more broadly, dumb women jokes. So obviously I was a child feminist; few things made me madder than being taken less than seriously. I loved learning in ways that few people around me did, and I was little-girl-splainer from way back. I read an entry in our set of encyclopedias after dinner every night. When my paternal grandfather—a biology teacher—remarked that I ate like a bird, I responded, "Actually, some birds eat their weight every day."

At that time, there were dual—and dueling—pop culture narratives about who feminists were. On the anti-feminism side, feminists were portrayed as hairy-legged lesbians (ain't a thing wrong with that) who hated men. On the pro-feminism side, feminists were portrayed as middle-class white women who no longer wanted to be shackled to the domestic realm; this position assumed that the women had grown up in *Leave it to Beaver* households and were expected to run similar ones. Either way, feminists were portrayed as deadly serious, right down to the stern correction of "Ms." (For a number of years, I thought that was the formal way to address divorced women, in the same way I believed "God damn it" was the formal way of saying "Damn it" or "Damn.")

———

Neither of the narratives about feminists sat right with me. I knew there was a difference between wanting respect and lacking a sense of humor.

Mom was, and is, funny. As a kid, I interrupted her while she was doing something requiring attention, like balancing the checkbook. "When can we start swearing?" I asked.

"When you're twenty-one," she said absentmindedly.

I went back to whatever I was doing—reading my Nancy Drews, goofing off in the yard, writing stories— and something occurred to me. I went back to her. "When did *you* start swearing?"

"When I was twenty," she said without looking up.

"Then why do we have to wait until we're twenty-one?" I asked.

She looked me in the eyes and said in full sincerity, "I regretted swearing that whole year."

And she certainly didn't have a *Leave It to Beaver* childhood.

———————

During the summers between her college years, Mom worked at Mayview, a mental institution where her mother and grandmothers worked.

The hospital began as a poorhouse for the city of Pittsburgh—originally named Marshalsea for the legendary debtor's prison in London where Charles Dickens's father had been imprisoned—and it also housed the mentally ill, the mentally disabled, unmarried pregnant women, and patients with tuberculosis. The 335-acre site once had a full-fledged farm and coal mine worked by the residents; it was a self-sustaining village, really, with the patients/debtors providing the labor. (The poorhouse aspect was phased out in 1958, and starting in 1975, patients were no longer allowed to work on the farm.)

Mom worked in admissions. One day, a patient attacked her, choking Mom with the love beads on Mom's neck, convinced that her husband had given them to Mom. The elevator opened and an orderly rushed to save Mom. (She went on a date with him. He was lovely, a vet, but he had a drinking problem.)

Her coworkers were a mixed bunch. Some wanted to punish her for being a college girl. To them, Mom's decision to go to college meant she thought she was better than them. She didn't—she just didn't want a life working at Mayview or the other offerings in her hometown. Other coworkers wanted to shield her from the worst of Mayview and the heartbreak that came with it. She didn't escape the heartbreak, though. Patients like the woman whose sitter baked her baby in the oven were beyond Mom's ken as a young woman, but she looked out for the kids. A fourteen-year-old boy lived on and off at Mayview, his parents unable to care for him, but he pinned his hopes on an uncle in Ohio. While the uncle didn't come through, Mom brought him magazines, candy, and gum; all she could offer, really, was her friendship.

She also volunteered at Morganza, officially known as Western Center, a facility for juvenile delinquents and disabled children. She developed a relationship with Bobby, who was six or seven when Mom first met him during her high school years. "I think now he might have been mildly autistic," Mom told me. "He just seemed so lost. I'd see him in the summers when I went to college. Over spring break, I'd bring him home for Easter." She was just a teenager herself, though, and one forging an unfamiliar path.

By the time my parents married in 1971, when she was twenty-two and he was twenty-one, they agreed that Dad would bring in the money so Mom could stay home with us, a luxury her foremothers didn't have. None of my family history squared with the popular narratives of feminism, positive or negative. While the history books record women taking back the right to work, Mom was finally taking back the right to raise her children without leaning on them to raise each other.

Pop history—and nostalgia—ignores that version of second-wave feminism.

In high school, I found my first legitimate response to second-wave feminism. In my English class, we'd read Alice Walker's *The Color Purple*, and I checked out Walker's other books from the library. One was *In Search of Our Mothers' Gardens*, first published in 1983, a collection of Walker's nonfiction. Walker introduced me to the term "womanist." She defined it as:

> A woman who loves other women, sexually and/ or nonsexually. Appreciates and prefers women's culture, women's emotional flexibility . . . and

women's strength. . . . Committed to survival and wholeness of entire people, male *and* female. Not a separatist, except periodically, for health. . . . Loves music. Loves dance. Loves the moon. *Loves* the Spirit. . . . Loves struggle. *Loves* the folk. Loves herself. *Regardless.* . . . Womanist is to feminist as purple is to lavender.

I couldn't call myself a womanist—that belonged to Black culture. But for a couple years after reading that, I went around declaring myself a "humanist," completely unaware that the term didn't mean what I thought it meant. But I wanted something more expansive. I wanted something that validated my foremothers' narratives.

By the time I went to college in 1990, the pop culture narratives had changed. On the anti-feminism side, radio host Rush Limbaugh introduced the world to the term "feminazi" in 1992. After some debate—and women-bashing—Congress approved Clarence Thomas's Supreme Court nomination, even after he clearly harassed Anita Hill. Television and radio brought us sexist boors like Howard Stern, Andrew Dice Clay, and Adam Carolla.

But during that time, third-wave feminism was born. Musically, all genres that I listened to embraced women's music, from hip-hop to grunge to pop to. . . well, I don't know what it's technically called, but I'd categorize it as torch songs for emotionally unavailable men. Fashion-wise, we were released from the clutches of brands so popular in the eighties. It was a strange time to be a young woman. I really can't overstate how hard condoms were emphasized. HIV was untreatable at that point, and the mother of my first-year roommate stocked our room with condoms. To a lesser degree, we got an earful about rape, and our resident advisor in the dorms warned us to steer clear of certain fraternities known for preying on women fresh out of high school.

To be a feminist at that time meant possibly being sex-positive but always being very fucking careful.

The University of Virginia in the early nineties felt very much like most of the students had read *The Official Preppy Handbook* as a Bible. In a socially conservative environment, alternative culture was, even with all its warts—and I'm looking at the guys who engaged in a pissing contest about who could champion the most obscure music—a lens to a social life that didn't include the white Greek scene with the vagina-drying phrase, "date functions."

Academically, I majored in English and came pretty close to earning a Women's Studies minor. I loved my professors, who were, by my third year, mostly women. I learned about women poets, fiction writers, and scientists. I read works by women from many different ethnic and cultural backgrounds. I read a goodly amount of work by writers who were lesbians. But in the academy, I didn't learn a thing about American working-class women: the maid that my great-grandmother had once been, the psychiatric technician my grandmother once became (after studying for the test with four children at home), the first-generation college student training to teach that my mother was. The helping jobs—historically done by women—were erased in favor of professional women trailblazers. I'm not saying this was wrong. But it wasn't necessarily right either.

I call Mom and tell her that our house was the preferred place to hang when I was a teenager.

"I liked *your* friends," she says.

"And we know what happens when you don't like them," I say. "Just ask David."

Mom laughs. When one of my sisters was in middle school, she had some friends over. David said something rude about Mom. He was one of those preteens who was all teeth, bones, and thinks-he's-cute attitude. Mom, five foot ten, picked him up, carried him to the front stoop, deposited him there, and locked the door. All the while, he protested, "I was just kidding! Let me back in!"

"Go home, David."

Mom modeled how to demand respect, but she also modeled how to support women. Several times, she opened her home to young women who needed help but couldn't get it from their own families. They ranged from a teenager whose parents were too messed up to properly care for her to a young mother and her baby whose partner abused her. I was an adult by then, but she's advocated for young people her whole life.

One of my earliest memories of her kindness: Mom gave away the flower girl dresses Erin and I had worn to our aunt and uncle's wedding to another mother who was marrying her children's father and who couldn't afford to buy something special for her own girls. As a teacher, she conscripted us to volunteer in her classrooms when we were old enough, and when a student's family couldn't afford proper clothes—one kid came to school dressed in cutoff men's jeans with a rope for a belt—she went shopping for a new wardrobe, giving the clothes to the principal to distribute. She knew what it was like to be poor, and she knew what prejudices individual students would face once they grew, and she tailored how she interacted with them to their needs. When parents insisted that their child needed a male teacher to rein that child in, her principal told them that he'd put Ms. Niesslein up against any male teacher and she'd win. I lost track of how many times she's been invited to gatherings to honor high school seniors as their most important teacher.

I think in every field, feminism needs several tracks to elevate women. The trailblazers most definitely have their place. But what gets lost in second-wave feminism are the uncelebrated women who've changed the world for the better, person by person.

It still gets lost, and the nostalgic narrative has no room for nuance. Nostalgia relies on a certain kind of shorthand that, for most people, plucks the attention-grabbing headlines and images from history. It will always elevate the mainstream over the marginalized, the broad over the detailed. Even now, I see how Tarana Burke didn't get credit for coining #MeToo in the early days of the movement. I see how slowly older women embraced intersectionality. Hell, I see my own faults in failing to seek out writers with less power than me in the publications I've helmed.

I don't want to be the older person who looks at the nation's phobias and -isms like a knotted necklace and thrusts it into the hands of someone younger and with better eyesight. "Here, I did what I could—fix it, would you?" But I take inspiration from younger activists who didn't have to unlearn racism and classism and sexism and ableism and machismo. Or didn't have to unlearn it as much as I did. Many of them came to the conclusion that human rights are interconnected at a far younger age than I did. We all need potable water. We all need safety from violence. We all need justice. We all need a living wage. We all need respect.

I asked Mom a couple years ago why exactly she wants "Respect" played at her funeral.

"Because respect is important to me," she said. "And it's a fun song. *I'm* fun."

Oh, Mom. Sock it to me, sock it to me, sock it to me.

NEW GALILEE

The light is getting progressively stranger the closer we come to peak eclipse.

It's August 2017, and my husband, Brandon, and I are driving our son, Caleb, from our home in Virginia to Oberlin Conservatory, where Caleb will attend college. The three of us are antsy in the rented minivan packed with all of Caleb's stuff, including eight instruments, the luggage we bought him for high school graduation, and a mug he plucked from the cupboard. In twenty-four hours, he'll no longer live at home—my wavy-haired boy, my earnest boy, my beloved boy.

"There," I say to Brandon. "Take this exit."

I'm the only one of us familiar with this route, and then only in a weird childhood-memory way, tunneling down through the layers of my life. The stretch of highway in western Pennsylvania leading us to Oberlin is a *This-Is-Your-Life* tour for me: Uniontown, where I was born; Muse, where my maternal grandparents lived; Sewickley, where my paternal grandparents lived; New Galilee, where I grew up.

I haven't been here since I was eleven years old, a little girl studying the Pennsylvania Turnpike card in the backseat, crammed against my sisters. "Turn right, away from Beaver Falls," I say to Brandon. We get to the stoplight where my classmate's dad owned a bar. "Left here," I say, as if in a dream.

There it all is—the route my bus took after my elementary school closed; the place that had the "Fill Dirt Wanted" sign; the bend in the road where we saw Charlie No-Face; the scary drop-offs that now have guardrails. And then things look unfamiliar for a stretch. "Are you sure this is the way? That's a really long bus ride," Brandon says.

"Just go a little farther. If I'm right, there'll be houses, then a stop sign." The houses—where my best friend lived, where my mom's first New Galilee friend lived—appear. The stop sign appears. We take a left.

The partial eclipse will happen soon. We'd planned to pull over when it happened so we could watch it through our paper and cellophane glasses.

I guide Brandon to the small driveway that leads to New Galilee Community Park. "I can't believe you remember this," he says. We ease the minivan to a stop near the bike rack where, long ago, my dad took a photo of my sisters and me. I look down at the dirt—a dark brown—and think: *I'm finally home.*

It's a strange thought. I only lived in New Galilee for five years and change—ages five to eleven—but to my mind, New Galilee was my entire childhood. I remember being five years old, sitting frog-legged near the grapevines, staring up at the clouds and thinking that I was lucky to land here, in this family, as if there had been some cosmic lottery.

In 1977, I moved with my parents, my three-year-old sister, Erin, and newborn Krissy into a house built in 1889, a former Presbyterian manse. It was a beautiful house. The upper panel of our front door was made of stained glass, bubbled with age. Strangers would knock and offer to buy it off the hinges. Great-Grandma Crawford—then in her seventies—came over to hang new wallpaper in the stairwell, and my mother hung white sheers in the sunroom that billowed when a breeze kicked up; the girls and I listened to K-Tel records, lying on the carpet.

Our decor on Locust Street was distinctly seventies, but the bones of the house were old; I can still feel the worn softness of the banister's wood under my palms, smell the dirt floor of the root cellar. We had a two-story garage in the back where Dad used the mechanic's pit to rebuild an old car. I'd bring him iced sun tea that Mom brewed. Sometimes I'd explore the second floor, hoping to magically find lost treasures—it was always just toys we'd outgrown.

New Galilee was a fire hall town—that's where all the social events took place. The kids' scout meetings were usually held there, and the adults organized dances and other events for themselves. Every summer, the carnival set up in the fields behind it. One time my dad won "Best Legs" at a fire hall shindig for the grown-ups. In my mind, it was just further proof of my luck. Dad had the best legs and my mom, the PTA president, was the prettiest mom of all of the girls' moms in my class. I could be a mouthy little thing, but I knew not to lord my good fortune over the other kids, what with their mediocre-legged fathers and average mothers.

One night, Dad brought home an Atari set. The next day, Mom and Dad both took the day off—Mom was back to teaching by now—and we were all home. Mom was big on "mental health days" for us girls. The wood-burning stove gave off cozy heat. (Erin had gotten in trouble sometimes for melting crayons on it, but the worst

I'd done was dip my finger in the pot of well water that was meant to keep the room humidified; I'd watch it sizzle on the surface, leaving mineral traces behind.) I got the hang of the joystick and eventually became really good at Space Invaders. I leaned against my parents, both cross-legged on the floor. Our nest of Niessleins reconfigured every once in a while as we took turns. A warm jumble.

But arriving back here in my hometown in 2017, this is the memory that clings to me: I'm on my bike, sailing around New Galilee. I sail through the entire town. The wind tangles my hair into reddish, brown-gold knots. I stand up on my pedals and glide down Washington Street until I need to pump again. For once, my sisters aren't on the banana seat with me or perched on the handlebars. I'm free, I'm free, I'm free, and the whole town is mine.

———————

It didn't last, of course—no childhood does, even (or especially) an idyllic one. It was the early eighties, and forces beyond our control were at work. Pittsburgh had lost its steel jobs years ago, but counties like ours, on the far periphery, were now starting to feel the decline of the entire industry, with the introduction of Japanese steel and foreign-made cars. Now, I have a better understanding of what happened, but that's about all I could figure as a kid. At nine years old, though, I felt one of the immediate effects: the closing of our elementary school due to budget cuts. The fourth-grade New Galilee kids were bussed to Koppel, another small town nearby. In that first year, I don't think any of us integrated well, either with the Koppel kids or the staff, who were so unlike our own warm elementary school teachers, some of whom wound up at Big Beaver Elementary along with the younger kids.

My new teacher, Mr. Martin, was one of the coldest. One afternoon, after an indoor recess, he flashed the lights and we quieted. I quieted last. I'd been teasing my friend David. I'd envied him, back in New Galilee, because he got to see his grandma every school day; she'd been our janitor. That day in Koppel, I'd called him a "fart." Mr. Martin looked at me and slapped a wooden paddle against his hand. I found my mouthiness from home: "You can't paddle me. My mom wrote a note." He reddened and let it drop.

The next year, we fifth graders were bussed to Beaver Falls Middle School. My dad, like a lot of other fathers, was laid off from his machinist job. In houses everywhere, brand-name foods were replaced by white bags and boxes with black lettering of what was inside. The kids at school started using "generic" as an insult.

I didn't especially like Koppel or Beaver Falls, but I clung to New Galilee. Maybe everyone wants childhood to last as long as possible. Maybe I was scared by the new knowledge that a bigger world was out there, and I'd have to find my place in it.

When we left for Dad's new job in Virginia, I walked the sidewalks one last time, memorizing the cracks. I had vivid dreams for years about our house. When I was young and interested in things like astral projection, I wondered sometimes if the current inhabitants ever spied a spectral me late at night, my fingers light on the banister, my face glowing between the white Swiss dot curtain panels in my bedroom.

I wasn't the only person in my family who lived there, of course, and at least four of us were old enough to remember what it was like. My sister Erin went back a few years ago. She brought back loose stones from the retaining wall in front of the house for each of us, but she warned me against returning. "It's not like you remember," she said.

It isn't. In 2017, driving through the town and past the house, I realize it fit my childhood so well because it's a child-sized town. It takes all of ten minutes to pass through—and then only because we stop at the base of the old driveway, and a woman, mowing a lawn nearby, looks at us funny.

"Hey, stop," I say to Brandon.

I get out, painfully aware that I don't look small town anymore, with my cat-eye glasses and city clothes. Still, she's friendly. Her mom, who I don't remember, had lived in a house at the end of our driveway and died recently; she's prepping the house to sell.

We commiserate a bit about loss. I tell her that I lived in the house up the driveway when I was a girl. She doesn't remember us, but then again, she'd left home at that point. She gestures to the house. "Both their cars are there."

"Oh, I don't want to bother them."

"From what I hear, it's still like it was when they bought it back in the eighties. But they're . . . strange. They have dogs. They don't talk to anyone."

I'm okay with just the land and my memories.

Mom, Erin, and I have woven a collective myth of those perfect years. Mom says it was the happiest time in her life, and I believe her. She got to do what none of her foremothers could afford to: stay at home with her kids. Erin and I reminisce about the records we danced to in the sunroom and the time we scraped up the sand under the aboveground pool after Dad took it down for the season (we genuinely thought we might have made the world's biggest sand pile). We tag each other on Facebook with sweet sentimental pictures. Any hardships stay in the shade of the golden times.

———————

And then there's Dad. We stay with Dad and his wife, Lori, both on the way to Oberlin and on the way back. Their house is the halfway point, in what could be described as "the middle of nowhere."

On the way back, I sit on the deck overlooking the mountains and talk with Dad about the old times. We reminisce about those years: our fishing trip to Lake Erie, the time he put me on the back of his motorcycle for a short ride, when we went to the drive-in. I tell him we stopped in New Galilee and that I saw the house.

"I like how it was the 'junk room' with mice until you cleaned it out and it became my bedroom," I tease, thinking of the bunk beds that Erin and I shared before our younger sister, Krissy, got old enough to warrant her own bed.

"That place was infested with mice. I had traps all over that house," Dad says. "Our mortgage was about two-fifty a month, and sometimes I wondered how we were going to make that." He worked two jobs, one as a teacher, the other as a wrestling coach, then a machinist.

I tell him we drove past the house where he built an addition one summer. "Still look good?" he asks.

"It looks great!"

He laughs. "The guy was all right, but I still had to deal with the wife. God, she was a pain in the ass."

"The kid used to try and lord it over Erin and me: 'Your dad's working for my dad!' I wondered what was wrong with her dad that he couldn't build his own addition."

We laugh. I pull on my newly purchased Oberlin sweatshirt, glad I bought something to warm me in the cold mountain air. Dad puffs on a cigar. "Moving from there was the best thing that ever happened to all of us."

I'm reluctant—so, so, reluctant—to make space for his memory alongside mine. I consider all that happened after we moved to Virginia, including the prolonged divorce that still leaves my sisters and me residually nervous when our parents have to be in the same room, even thirty years later. I give a little down-turned smile and don't say anything else. Memories don't have to match.

Later, though, I'll wonder if Dad was right. He spent those years working hard, and when that hard work dried up, he wasn't going to wait around. We had to move on for survival. And going back, I know for damn sure I wouldn't want to live in New Galilee as an adult. Although the town hasn't visually changed much—most everything is intact, though the population slipped from 624 in 1970 to 379 in 2010—my New Galilee only exists in my head.

You can—and I have—tie yourself in knots wondering what turns your life would have taken if one variable had been different. What if we'd never moved? Would I have itched for someplace bigger? Would I have met Brandon? Would I have watched the sky on August 21, 2017, in the same place, with the same people, with the same strange feelings?

I stand there in the New Galilee Community Park, in that weird light, watching the moon slide across the sun, and I think of my girl-self, so grateful that I ended up in my family. In that moment, I feel certain there were other possibilities—maybe in other potential lives, in other dimensions, on other planets, with the me-not-me looking up through cellophane and paper glasses at another eclipse.

But I'm here in this park, near the dark brown dirt that says *home*, staring at my very real eighteen-year-old son, and my very real forty-five-year-old husband, in the same wooden shelter where I made sit-upons as a Girl Scout, and I'm looking at the metal slide that I thought was so long when I was a kid and seeing the spinning barrel that scared me then—and I'm having a rare moment of seamlessness, the feeling that somehow Brandon and Caleb can really understand me now, seeing where I came from. I feel *whole*.

It's an illusion, I'll realize later; the next bit of this detour will have a distinct let's-humor-Mom scent to it. But for now, I'm caught up in the magic of two celestial bodies passing close enough that they seem to almost touch. In this moment, in this green summer park, it's the sun and the moon, but also the past and the present, the memory and the facts, the life I live now and the one I have yet to begin, with a freshly emptied bedroom in Virginia.

THE CENTER OF ANYTHING

*I distrusted, in general, appeals to nostalgia—I loved
the past of archives, but there was no era in the past I
had any inclination to revisit with my actual human
body, being rather fond of it having at least minimal
rights and protections.*

—Danielle Evans
The Office of Historical Corrections

I spent my tween and teen years in Sterling, Virginia.
When my parents told me we were moving to Virginia, I
had vague ideas of former plantations dotting the land and
classmates who talked like the cast of *Hee Haw*. I wondered
how I would fit in. The idea of being a northerner in the
South was the thing that worried me. It somehow escaped
my attention that my unfashionable perm—poodle on
top, ringlets in the back—and an old-style retainer that
caused me to slurp the saliva from the roof of my mouth
every few minutes might hinder the acclimation.

I didn't find the Old South in Sterling. What I found instead was an exurb of Washington, DC, with some strip malls and a few planned housing developments. We rented a house in a development called Sugarland Run, a community built in the 1970s boasting "California-style" homes. Ours, built in 1972, was the Laguna model. At eleven, and in 1983, everything about California seemed glamorous. (Swimming pools. Movie stars.) Less glamorous: the landlord who'd let himself in with no notice as if he had no concept of rent or privacy. He often didn't pay the HOA fees. On at least one occasion, my sisters and I were turned away at the community pool after presenting our delinquent cards, pissed, embarrassed, and overheated on the walk home in our flip-flops.

I got used to the sound of planes flying overhead, taking off and landing from Dulles Airport. My parents gave me the upstairs bedroom. It was the entire upper level of the house, but as soon as my youngest sister, Jill, grew out of her crib, I'd have to share it. My parents bought some particleboard furniture to create a quasi-separation. My roommates rotated between Erin and Krissy, depending on how much Erin and I were bickering.

By the time I graduated high school, Sterling held no charm for me whatsoever. I thought it a place without a center, not even a fire hall like in New Galilee. All of the interesting things to do—concerts, museums, plays, *life*—seemed to happen in bigger places. I skipped school with my friends to go to the Smithsonian museums in DC or the National Zoo. One friend and I used to go to Dulles at night—then off of a four-lane road with a stoplight—to watch planes take off out of the huge plate glass windows. I wished I were on them, flying to the center of anything.

My years in Sterling were probably the unhappiest of my life. Did I ever love it?

It started off okay. In middle school, I experienced some light bullying, but not really enough to keep my spirits down. The goofball in me came out strong—in health class, for example, I performed a rap about the dangers of inhalants to the tune of New Edition's "Cool It Now." I made friends, and some of them are still my friends today. I eventually blossomed from an ugly duckling into a regular duck, but by the time I was a high school sophomore, I was just over it all. Why couldn't everyone behave like adults and be treated with dignity? Why must there always be a ruckus?

The timing wasn't a coincidence. Sterling was where I grew from a girl to a young woman, and I can't overstate the sexism of the eighties or its effect on me. My high school felt very boy culture, all football and heavy metal and talk dirty to me. Girls were ornaments, the trophies, the afterthought. My freshman history teacher literally called one girl in my class "Mallory," referencing the ditzy sister in the TV show *Family Ties*. A guy a year older than me used to play basketball at our next-door neighbor's hoop what felt like constantly, harassing me whenever I left or came home. Sometimes Mom would send me to 7-11 to buy a staple we'd run out of; there was always a group of skeevy men in their twenties hanging out at pay phones who'd eye me up and down. "Milk and bread, that's what I said," one drawled at me as he gawked at whatever he thought he saw of my body under my baggy clothing. At school we were required to attend pep rallies—I know, standard-issue high school, but I seethed. The one school activity we were supposed to rally around—football— excluded girls, not to mention anyone in the drama club or the debate team. At Beaver Falls Middle School, I came in first to represent our team on Pittsburgh's "Kid's Quiz" on WTAE. At Broad Run High School, when I became a young woman, any intellectual recognition disappeared. I lived in a John Hughes movie, but in a way less affluent community.

My parents separated when I was fifteen. I knew it was coming; my bedroom vent was above their bedroom—their arguments and the general tension in the house didn't escape me. It was a typical suburban boomer breakup, and I was mostly concerned about the financial impact on me. "I'm not going to give up my lifestyle!" I proclaimed to my parents. Credit cards were available to people like my parents now, and we'd just recently graduated from buying clothes from stores that also sold rat poison to stores that had paid perfume spritzers. All the suburban kids with parents involved in a contentious divorce reacted in different ways. Me, I grew a hard emotional shell and got an after-school job, and then another on top of the first one—you know, to support my lifestyle.

For a very long time, I considered the whole of Sterling as somewhere that existed for me to resent—an anti-nostalgic time and place—for these reasons. And for what became of Sterling later.

———

Sterling's located in eastern Loudoun County, arguably the richest county in the United States. It doesn't matter which metric you use—annual income (number one) or total wealth (number twenty-five). The distribution of wealth in the US is famously uneven; it's just writ large in eastern Loudoun, where my mother taught both homeless children and ones whose parents could collectively afford, say, a professional coach's salary for their kids' soccer team.

It wasn't always this way. When I lived in Sterling, I'd see bumper stickers that read, *Don't Fairfax Our Loudoun.* Fairfax, the next county over, epitomized suburbia: strip mall after shopping center after apartment complex after subdivision. No center existed there either, but the traffic was worse and there wasn't any green space I was aware of, except maybe Lake Anne, where there was a French restaurant Mom took me to on my sixteenth birthday.

Can you call it gentrification if most of what you remember still exists?

I'm going to commit to a yes. Living in Sterling is expensive. My parents bought our house for $86,000 in 1985—that's about $205,500 today. Thanks to the influx of money into the area, though, the house isn't worth that. It's worth, according to realtor.com, $552,700. Granted, Erin renovated the upstairs to share the house with Mom, but if you knock off a hundred grand, it's still more than double what the house would be worth if no one had Fairfaxed our Loudoun.

Sugarland Run occupies a weird socioeconomic place in Sterling, both then and now. Idyllic or lowbrow? Depends who you ask.

On one hand, you can find social media groups dedicated to the nostalgia of growing up in Sugarland. Even our high school's most famous alumnus, Patton Oswalt, mentioned Sugarland in his graduation speech for Broad Run High School a few years ago: "I was living in Sugarland Run, whose motto is, "Ooooh! A bee! Shut the door!" He also wrote a goodly amount about Sterling in his book *Zombie Spaceship Wasteland*.[1]

And then there's the other hand. When the newer housing developments were built in the mid-1980s, I didn't think anything of it. Countryside. Seneca Ridge. Cardinal Glen. These houses weren't especially fancier, just newer, and a lot of families who'd lived in Sugarland just picked up the furniture from their Sugarland houses and moved into them. When I visited friends in the newer subdivisions, they seemed as comfortable and open as my own house.

1 If you went to Broad Run High School in the eighties, you're obligated to talk about Patton Oswalt. He did the morning announcements when he was a senior and I was a freshman. The first time I saw him on TV, it was on Comedy Central, back when the programming consisted of stand-up comedians performing in front of a wall. I tried to place where I'd seen him. "I think he dated someone famous," I said to Brandon, next to me on the love seat in our college hovel. He'd actually dated the school nurse's daughter. So that's my bar for famous. I hear tell of BRHS alumni renting a bus to see him perform when he's in DC.

But by the time I was a senior in the fall of 1989, developers had built expensive, grander houses on the farmland around my high school, land that used to earn us the nickname "Cornfield High." Uh oh, I thought. One thing BRHS had going for it was its (more or less) economic homogeneity. My parents and my friends' parents had jobs and careers that earned them enough money for lower-middle-class to middle-class lives: teachers, mechanics, salespeople. Lots of government employees. (It was an unspoken rule that if someone's parent worked for the government, you didn't ask in what capacity. In my preteen and teen imagination, there were *a lot* of FBI and CIA operatives driving their kids to track practice and making Price Club runs in their off time.) I didn't know what these new people who lived in "Ashburn Farms" and "Ashburn Villages" did for a living, but showing off their wealth, I thought, was definitely a hobby.

I'd seen economic disparity before, and I didn't like this influx of money—no one has a more acute sense of social class dynamics than an adolescent in the greed-is-good eighties who owns a "Shrap" calculator. I'd be out of the area soon, but I worried for my younger sisters. We already had a fairly wealthy uncle who treated us like the help. I babysat my cousins for a pittance, and he hired Erin and Krissy—maybe ten and seven years old at the time—to do lawn work and then complained about the results. What do little kids know about lawn work?

I think we were supposed feel grateful for these "opportunities," as if hiring cheap child labor were a version of generosity. I imagined whole neighborhoods of this uncle infiltrating the area, treating us with the same condescension.

My wariness wasn't unwarranted. My sister Krissy and a friend I'll call Christy were called to court after hanging out with another friend who, later in the day, hung out with still another friend who shot a gun. Christy's father forbade her to come to Sugarland any more, as if the neighborhood had suddenly become *The Godfather* set in real life.

Years later, when I was in college, my sister Jill joined a youth softball league. Mom joined the sidelines with the other parents to cheer the kids on. "Are you from the Villages or the Farms?" another parent asked her.

She replied drily, "The Run."

I left Sterling with little nostalgia for it, either the original version or the version I saw coming down the pike. Yet twenty years after my departure, I attended my class reunion. I don't know what I was thinking.

Geographically, I didn't make it very far from Sterling. I live just a few hours away by design, because I never wanted to be very far from Mom and my sisters. In high school, I thought I'd live in New York City at some point, the touted center of everything. That didn't happen; I live in the same city where I went to college. Emotionally, though, I'd traveled a million miles from the unhappy teenager who hailed from The Land of a Thousand Beefs. By the time I was thirty-eight, I had nothing at all to complain about on a personal level. I was happily married with a thriving business, a child we adored, cherished friends and family. I wanted to see my friends from my high school years. (I had friends! I wasn't *totally* insufferable.) We made a loose arrangement to meet up.

Brandon and I drove west to Leesburg to a dive bar that had been there forever. I assumed the reunion organizers chose this bar over the many better-smelling options now in Sterling out of some type of nostalgia.

Happily, I laced fingers with Brandon as we walked through the parking lot. At the hostess stand, some former classmates waited to greet the class of 1990 with Mardi Gras beads in our school colors. There, our class's homecoming queen seemed not to recognize me. When I told her my name, she said, "Oh, you used to have long hair!"

"Yes," I said. "I did."

So that's how the evening started out. It felt . . . very high school.

Brandon and I made our way through the dim bar, and I ran into two guys I knew. After I'd introduced them, we chatted about nothing while Brandon got us some drinks. One guy had a way of raising his eyebrows when he laughed that, when we were kids, made me suspect he was making fun of me. Turns out, that's just the way he laughs.

I wandered around with Brandon, making small talk with people I recognized from Facebook. I know: many a think piece has sprung forth about how social media makes people feel inferior. For me, though, when someone from my past friend-requested me, it felt like a little friendly way of saying, "Hello! I remember your existence!" Which was nice, at least in the beginning, and no one from my past has ever embraced the humblebrag.

Social media has also paved the way for me to see some of my former classmates as their adult selves. These were some of the bright spots: Cerise, funny and down-to-earth; Heather, whip-smart and married to a guy Brandon and I made fast friends with; Jeff B., who took all the same classes I did, though we didn't really know each other until we connected on social media where he showed his wit and kindness. And of course, Beth—we've been friends for what feels like forever, and we hugged each other tight.

I tethered myself to these lovely souls because they tethered me to my happy adult self. But I didn't totally glom on to them—they'd had their own high school experiences and the right to reconnect with their other friends. Occasionally, I wandered to the bar or outside, and I bumped into classmates. Individually, they all seemed like perfectly nice people. They addressed me as "Jenny," a name only family and close friends use now. It was jarring. More jarring, though, was looking at the group from a booth where I chatted with Brandon and two other spouses. Gathered in this oppressively loud bar, I couldn't separate the alumni group from what I associated them with. I felt myself slipping into my resentful teenage self.

I woke up the day after, dreading the next leg of the reunion. It was eleventy gazillion degrees outside, and the organizers had scheduled us at an outdoor park in Leesburg, J. R.'s Festival Lakes. Some other stab at nostalgia for the old version of Loudoun, I supposed. I'd been there one time for my dad's company picnic when I was twelve. It was one of the few green spaces still left in eastern Loudoun, albeit a commercial one. I had to go, though. I'd initiated the meetup for my high school friends.

Dressing, I rejected a sundress as too revealing for this crowd and wound up wearing all black. When it's eleventy gazillion degrees, it turns out it doesn't really matter— you're going to roast anyway.

I met up with my friend Andrea and her family, and I met up with Beth. The facility brought out some, by anyone's standards, mediocre food and some kegs of Bud. I kept waiting for the arrival of Janie, my best friend from high school, and Jeff H., who I once considered something like a brother. Andrea and her family went home, defeated by heat. Brandon went to hang out with Heather's husband after a time, braving the mosquitos in the woods. Janie, with an infant at home, stayed in Texas, and I can't say I blamed her.

By the time Jeff H. got there, I was sweaty and verging on cranky. I was happy to see him, this long-lost like-a-brother, but it was time to go. We made plans to meet up back in Sugarland at my old home, where after an ice-cold shower, I knew I could be my normal self.

———

In the thirty years since I left, I mostly stuck close to Mom and Erin's house when I visited. Although it's been remodeled and undergone some construction, it's still a home away from home, even down to the way it smells: a mix of Lemon Pledge, Windex, and Lysol underneath the smell of Mom's baking (brownies with peanut butter chips if you're lucky).

In the ten years since the reunion, the changes keep barreling on. J. R.'s Festival Lakes is now a deforested housing development. The retail space next to the video/porn store where I worked is a delicious Burmese restaurant. Even at the house, the place where I used to lie my teenage head to sleep is now a wet bar.

The changes are larger than the details, though. The demographics of the area have shifted.

Sugarland Run itself is no longer majority white. The majority of the children at the school my sisters attended, Sugarland Run Elementary, are Hispanic or Latinx. My niece's sixteenth birthday party looked like one of those old United Colors of Benetton ad shoots. Both the older and newer parts of Sterling are far more diverse than they used to be, and, as a result, my white nephew and niece are much better equipped to deal with the larger world than I ever was, and they won't have to unlearn otherizing.

The real divide in Sugarland isn't racial but economic. Often it comes down to who's an owner in residence and who rents their property out. Walking her dog on the paths behind the houses and townhouses, Erin tells me most of the houses and yards are well-kept. In some of the townhouses, she sees restored siding and paint from new homeowners. In others, she sees homes where the renters are powerless to combat the rotting siding ignored by the owners.

The feel of the community varies street by street. On Mom's street, it's mostly the same. She's been there the longest, but the neighbors still value the community they've developed. In the 2016 national election, she and a neighbor with antichoice stickers plastered on his car wound up at the polls at the same time as Margot, a neighbor who'd immigrated. Both Mom and the neighbor hung out to make sure no one hassled Margot about casting her ballot. They look out for each other.

For years, I thought that Broad Run's twentieth reunion and the locations the organizers chose represented some sort of nostalgia for the worst of what Loudoun was back when I lived there—the sexism, the racism, the coded homophobia, the anti-intellectualism. The sort of oppressive nonsense I hoped to escape to in a place with a center.

But I was talking to Erin over a recent Thanksgiving weekend, telling her my theory. Erin and Jeff, my brother-in-law, had attended the reunion, too. She was wiping down the kitchen while the turkey I'd stuffed was roasting. "That bar was picked because somebody's sister worked there," she said. "We wound up at that park because it was cheap."

Oh.

The problem with my own anti-nostalgia for Sterling is that it never evolved. If nostalgia acquires a burnished glow over the years, anti-nostalgia stays stagnant and grows fetid. I'd hung on to my twin resentments for what Sterling was and what it became for so long that I'd completely ignored that the house in Sugarland remains ground zero for so many of my memories of joy with my sisters and mother, husband and son, niece and nephews.

No one in the newer developments in Sterling is actually trying to fight Sugarland Run, unless you count the oddly pretentious people who put "Potomac Falls" as their return mailing address when the zip code is plain old Sterling. Fun fact: the Trump National Golf Club claims its location as Potomac Falls, although it has a Sterling zip code. There was another, more recent push to change the zip entirely so the Lowes Island subdivision could be renamed "Potomac." That didn't fly.

As far as I can tell, that's about the extent of the snobbery of eastern Loudoun's newer residents. There's not animosity, according to some of my friends still in the area. It's more like Sugarland Run has just been disappeared from Sterling's collective mind. As one of my friends told me, they just shop at the newer stores, live in the newer houses, paying no mind to what and who existed before.

I was clicking through the *Washington Post* one afternoon when the headline "Sugarland Run: Trails, trees, and much more in a pocket near the Potomac" caught my attention. The article touted the development's affordability—over a half-million dollars for a single family home. One resident, who'd been in Sugarland since 2007, told the reporter, "We love the location. It doesn't matter which direction I want to go—toward D.C., toward Leesburg—it's right in the center. It is close to everything."

I thought then of my teenage self, yearning to jump on a plane to the center of anything, wanting so much for my real life to begin. I'm deep into my real life now. I've been to New York City—that touted center of everything—a handful of times, and I can tell you, it doesn't have a center either. Real life is where you live it. Sometimes there are gigantic planes flying overhead. Sometimes the brownies are baking. Sometimes there are your beloveds crowded around a karaoke machine in a Sugarland Run sitting room. The center is you.

SO HAPPY TOGETHER

We met in a dim basement. The fraternity—we can't remember which, any one of those old columned houses lining Rugby Road—pumped music so loud we had to shout in each other's ears to be heard. We were refilling our red Solo cups from the keg of cheap beer when we first yelled to each other. We were dressed alike, in T-shirts and denim shorts. We joked later that we found each other because we were the two people who looked as if they shouldn't be there, vaguely alternative kids in a sea of khakis and L. L. Bean.

We were nineteen years old. It's funny to think that we danced that night—we're not dancing people, we know now. We went outside to talk and stood close to each other. We didn't want the night to end so we piled in with the others in Kathy's little Honda; we slept in the same room that night, one of us in the bed, the other on the futon. From that night on, we were inseparable.

We both lost weight that first year. We woke each morning giddy that something good would happen that day: we would see each other. Of course, in the first few weeks, we were both a little cautious, consumed with a heady mix of romance and doubt. Was it completely reciprocal? Would we run out of things to talk about? Would some terrible, deal-breaking flaw reveal itself?

A kiss tamped the doubts down. We were walking from a party, holding hands for the few blocks to get to the convenience store. We were going to buy a pack of cigarettes. We stopped and turned toward each other, savoring those seconds when our mouths were near but hadn't yet made contact, the salty scent of our faces, the delicious nerves. We kissed. After that, we threw out caution. We took a sort of ownership of each other's bodies, a jumble of legs and arms and mouths and love.

On the university grounds, there was another couple that looked like us, her tall and with a sheet of long brown hair, him taller with a mop of curls. They broke up before graduation, but we wondered if they got the same sort of comments we did. A woman with a mental illness, who did somersaults on the pedestrian mall, told us that we were going to make beautiful children; strangers we'd just met would remark on how well matched we were. Our chemistry seemed like a force field.

We twined our lives together. We stood together outside the hospital room door and heard the first cries of our oldest nephew after his birth. We took cheap vacations to off-season Chincoteague, using our last ten in cash to cross the Chesapeake Bay Bridge Tunnel. We stayed up late, waiting for the other to get off shift waiting tables or tending bar. One summer day, we skipped work to go hiking at Sugar Hollow. It was a ways out of town and we drove with the windows open and the music pouring from the speakers. We found an easy, sun-dappled trail that led through some streams, and we walked the gentle incline, bumping into each other just as an excuse to touch skin. We took pictures of each other posing on a rock that lay just beneath the surface of the water, an optical illusion of levitation.

That's how we felt about each other: we each walked on water.

We grew up, shape-shifting together, holding hands like the Wonder Twins. We were the engineering major and the English major, who morphed into the trumpet player and the local journalist, and then turned into the chemical engineer and the aspiring short-story writer. We became husband and wife, father and mother, fly fisherman and Scrabble addict, quality assurance engineer and business owner.

We can see our flaws now, both in ourselves and each other. On the eve of our thirteenth wedding anniversary, a strong thunderstorm blew into town. A huge limb fell off our maple, hitting the yard with such force that it stuck into the earth at a forty-five degree angle. Worse, the city sewage line backed up into our basement.

We spent most of the night on the phone, calling the city and the sort of companies that clean up murder scenes. It was certainly grisly down there, the pipe in the recesses near the hot water heater spewing whole neighborhoods' worth of filth. We rolled a dampened towel and placed it under the basement door so the smell wouldn't permeate the rest of the house.

The next day, the city came to clear the wreckage, and the cleaning company came back to scour. We were tired and both missing work to deal with this minor catastrophe. After everyone left, we sighed, assessing our lost belongings— the antique chest that held sports equipment, a basket of laundry, the bright ceramic flowerpots bought on a long-ago Mother's Day. Our Christmas tree and ornaments, including every one that our son had ever made and the Lenox china one of two doves, bearing in gold script, "First Christmas Together 1991."

"Did you at least save the ornament—our ornament?" one asked the other.

"No—the whole box was disgusting."

Exhausted, we snapped then, reverting to type: one of us irritated and pragmatic, the other seething and sentimental. We didn't speak for the rest of the day, not so much as a punishment but to avoid saying something that we couldn't unsay. We took a nap; we came to our senses by dinnertime. It was our anniversary, for God's sake. We had each other, even if our keepsakes, as we'd later put it, went down with the shit.

It's been so many years, we might well be the kind of people that some refer to as "smug marrieds." We don't know. Every partnership is a locked box, knowable only to the people in it. But we don't feel smug. We feel grateful for the constant accrual of all these minutes together—the winks across a crowded room, the ass-grab in the kitchen, the phone call from home, the car sex on a (whoops, not quite) deserted road, the arm to cling to at the funeral, the words that our son mispronounced when he was little.

Last year, we hit a milestone birthday. It sounds odd to say, but we don't know what the other looks like anymore. We have too many associations—love, passion, comfort—to see one another with any degree of objectivity.

This is the age when people like us start to realize that they're out of big beginnings. Unless something unexpected happens, there will be no new romances, no new weddings, no more of your own babies to nuzzle. You know very well that you're not going to relocate.

Couples around us have started to break apart, tender bands of skin on their ring fingers, new apartment keys on their key chains. Even in the very best of circumstances—amicable, mutually decided, no kids—we find it sad for them, something with such a hopeful beginning coming to a close. No matter how much better off our friends wind up—and they are, they always are, at least emotionally—there is pain.

On a more self-involved level, though, these breakups remind us of something every couple loses sight of: that it only takes one of you to develop an itch for something new, and there is nothing at all that the other can do about it. It's the lesson we learn from our newly single friends over and over. We try hard to lose sight of the lesson for the sake of ourselves. As someone wise once said, "You gotta have faith, faith, faith."

We got married on the grounds of a sprawling bed and breakfast, just beyond the koi pond. It had sprinkled earlier in the day, but by the time the pianist struck up "Here Comes the Bride," the sky was clear and warm. We were twenty-four and wrote our own vows. The ceremony itself lasted all of five minutes.

It was a lovely beginning, but essentially it was just a party in celebration of us.

In novels and in jazz, the big squishy middle is where all of the interesting stuff happens. In our story, this is where we are now.

We don't know which events will seem important years down the road, but we're living the details right now. In our big, messy house, our son practices his clarinet. Our Boston terrier mix is still alive, goofy as ever. We haven't used a babysitter in a long while, and we usually go out to eat on Saturdays, just the two of us. We laugh ourselves silly over a random lyric we hear on the radio. We eat lunch together most days in the TV room and finish off with a piece of chocolate. One day in February, you come home from work with Chinese food for us, and I ask you, my valentine, to read this, and you do.

HOSPITALITY

As legend has it, the Homestead, a luxury resort in Bath County, Virginia, began when a guy reached the limits of his hospitality. George Washington deeded an army officer and head of a militia named Thomas Bullitt three hundred acres of land belonging to Indigenous people. Bullitt lived near the hot springs on this land, and once his friends got wind of it, they started visiting in droves, expecting him to foot the bill for their room and board. In 1766, a fed-up Bullitt built the first iteration of the Homestead. It's dizzying to get there today through twisty mountain roads, but in the eighteenth century, visitors had to endure two-day stagecoach rides on rough, rutted trails through the wooded mountains. In any case, the Homestead's older than the United States of America itself.

Two hundred and fifty years later, Brandon, Caleb, and I got our first glimpse of the Homestead. Caleb had secured a place in All-State Jazz, and the Homestead hosted the long weekend of intensive practice and performance. It's the sort of grand building that's meant to take your breath away the first time you see it, when you wind through the streets of Hot Springs, Virginia, until it's suddenly in view. Enormous, with a white-columned veranda, the hotel dominates the manicured landscape.

We weren't gazing at Bullitt's actual Homestead—the original wooden structure burned down in 1901 from a bakery fire, long after he sold it in the early 1800s. This Homestead dates from 1902, but the idea behind it is the same: upscale accommodations near the hot springs, exclusively for the people who can afford it.

———————

We come five days after Donald Trump won the electoral college vote to become president. We'd initially booked this stay on a lark. I figured that we could use a mini-vacation while Caleb did his thing, and I tend to turn every vacation into a field trip—this was an historic site, after all. But I get there predisposed to crankiness. Standing on the veranda, I think I might have made a big mistake. There's no getting around the plantation vibe of the Homestead, and I'm angry enough with conservative, rich white people as it is. In the grand lobby, white people mill about, preoccupied.

Sure, most of the younger ones are here for All-State Jazz, but I wonder how many of the older ones are looking for a let's-pretend-we're-plantation-owners experience. They're not going to get an authentic one.

———————

Bath County occupies a strange place in Virginia's history. Up until 1863, the county stood in what was then central Virginia. When part of the state seceded to become West Virginia, Bath County was suddenly a borderland. During the Civil War, some white men living there fought for the Union; others fought for the Confederacy. It was still the South, though. Many Black people were enslaved. The 1850 census was the first to include enslaved people in its "slave schedule," an attachment to the census itself, and the owner of the Homestead at the time, Dr. Thomas Goode, claimed an unnamed sixty-five Black people, ages two to eighty-five, as his property.

After the Civil War, many formerly enslaved people stayed put, their former owners becoming their employers.

It's completely understandable—what are you supposed to do without a penny to your name? But it also left the owners of the Homestead free to create a narrative in which, even after the Civil War, Black people were happily subservient to whites. One display near the front of the resort's library showcases the resort's culinary history. It includes a quote: "It's mighty nice to have you back at the Homestead." It's attributed to the late Woody Pettus, the maître d' of the main dining room since 1960. Pettus was a light-skinned Black man whose family has worked at the resort for five generations. He died two years after our visit, and the Homestead renamed one of its restaurants "Woody's" in his honor. But during our stay, the display didn't even include Pettus's photo—just the quote, a period table setting, and other memorabilia. What few photos of the staff that were displayed showed them at a distance, expressions unreadable, a sharp contrast to the portraits of the white patrons, closer, smiling and relaxed. It set my teeth on edge.

One store at the Homestead had Stan Cohen's book *The Homestead and Warm Springs Valley, Virginia: A Pictorial Heritage* (Quarrier Press, 1984) in stock. The book includes a photo of "Tray Races," in which the Black servants competed with metallic trays. From the picture, it appears the trays are balanced on their heads as white customers look on. The caption notes, "The event has since been discontinued." A 2014 article by the Block News Alliance syndicate quoted a long-time employee,

Arthur Bryan. "They had to stop because of the betting." According to the article, the tray races started in the 1940s and didn't end until 1965. White people were gambling on the speediness of the Black staff.

———————

The whole stay is an experience of cognitive dissonance.

"I don't belong here" has echoed around in my brain before. I've been an overnight guest in a famous actor's home, slept in her child's bed, chatted pleasantly with her. I visited a friend at her family's actual mountaintop castle, with staff quarters and everything. When my first book came out, a car waited outside my hotel—the valet held a sign with my name on it.

Each of these experiences felt surreal. It's not that I felt guilty or intimidated. I'd come a long way from my beloved grandparents who, in their hometown, were pillars of their community but somehow became too shy to check themselves into the fancy hotel in which we'd booked them for my wedding. I wound up checking them in. I'm uncertain if they'd ever checked themselves in anywhere except work.

These personal experiences were pleasant, dreamlike, and surreal. Nothing in my life had prepared me for any brush with luxury. Comfort, yes. But I'd never imagined a life in which, say, a movie star would have to learn my name.

"I don't belong here" would cling to me during my stay at the Homestead, too, but this was more a nightmare. I felt out of time, trapped in someone else's idea of nostalgia. Still, I brought this on myself. It's true that the Homestead was the venue for All-State, true that I was unaware of any other accommodations in the area. But it's also true we were paying for this bad dream.

The Omni now owns the Homestead. I have no idea what you had to pay before it became part of a chain, but almost nothing is free. It costs $300 a night to start with, but you also pay ten dollars a night for parking, whether or not you use the valet.

The only person I knew who'd ever stayed there, once, was my sister Krissy. "The spa is awesome," she told me. The Homestead was founded on its supposed healing waters (seventeen dollars a pop), and its spa services are an extension of them. Krissy likes a spa, the pampering and the massages and the human touch.

I don't. I don't like strangers touching me in general. And at the Homestead, I became increasingly uncomfortable with the commerce required of human interaction.

They offer plenty of activities. There's the spa and shopping for the ladies. For the gents, there's golf ($140 on the Old Course, $210 on the Cascades Course); falconry lessons ($99 to $149); skeet shooting (in the $65 an hour range); and plain old target shooting (a bargain at $10 an hour if you bring your own .22 and ammo). There's nothing that says, of course, that women can't golf or shoot, but like the old big box toy stores, the décor in the rooms where you sign up for activities are color-coded: pastels for the ladies, hunter greens and navy blues for the gents.

At first, Brandon and I consider the activities.

Falconry?

"I kind of want to do it," he says. "But mostly because I think it'd be cool to have a picture with a falcon on my arm." He strikes a patrician pose and I laugh.

Archery?

"You know, I remember being kind of good at it in high school. That might be fun," I say. I think for a minute. "But the string always hit my arm behind the leather guard and I got a shit-ton of bruises."

We consider the Segway tours— $70 per a person— but it's that weird November weather in Virginia where no one knows how to dress themselves. One day it's lightly rainy and the kind of cold that gets into your bones, and the next, you're about to burst into flames.

Instead, we mostly just hang out. I figure we can make it work. Brandon wants to hear the jazz, and I always have a book.

———

The Segways and some of the activities—a summertime lazy river, miniature golf, wintertime snowmobiling— are nods to the contemporary, but it struck me again and again that the Homestead was doomed by making itself into a modern resort, part of the Omni or not.

Its biggest draw is its history, but that history is also its biggest ick factor. Determined not to spend more money than I had to, I went back to the library while Brandon eavesdropped on the jazz practices happening in the other wing. The books weren't anything special—a lot of James Patterson and other vacation reads. But the walls were filled with portraits of conservatives who'd stayed at the Homestead: Billy Graham, Richard Nixon, Ronald Reagan.

Another frame, toward the back of the room, memorializes the time (December 1941 through June 1942) the Homestead served as an interment camp for

745 Japanese diplomats and their families. During World War II, the federal government figured that they'd treat the diplomats from the countries they were fighting well, in hopes that the American diplomatic counterparts would receive the same treatment until they could perform the old switcheroo. (In a gross understatement, American citizens of Japanese descent didn't receive this same consideration.)

The whole theme of the room reads to me as "Southern Hospitality." And I start to put my finger on what skeeves me out about the words "southern" and "hospitality" in concert. I have nothing against regular hospitality; when we first moved to northern Virginia, Mom thought people weren't raised right if you came over and weren't offered something to drink and eat, even it was a cup of tea and a Bisquick coffee cake they threw together a half-hour ago. That's just good manners.

It's the "southern" part that trips me up. I've lived in the South most of my life, and I know there are about as many ways to be southern as there are people. But I do have an issue with those who consider themselves southern gentility. They're the ones who have always benefited from reactionary policies, the ones for whom the system worked in the past—and, in coming years, for whom the system will work under the Trump administration. They're white and vote Republican. They follow some unspoken rulebook that I don't really understand. As far as I can tell, it means no trendy clothes, just expensive preppy ones. No swearing, no smoking. Mingling with their own kind. Living so insularly as to render the rest of the world invisible; it's a very I-got-mine ethos. In the coming days, I'll be rendered invisible at the Homestead. I didn't grow up on the social radar of southern gentility. My whiteness isn't enough for the southern gentility.

It is enough, though, to make me realize that this flavor of "southern hospitality" means that my comfort will come at someone else's expense. Even today, even when staffers are paid. Just because something becomes a reenactment doesn't mean the original tragedy didn't occur. I trudge away from the library in disgust, whether with the Homestead— where nothing honorable is memorialized, where slavery doesn't even get a scant mention—or with myself for staying here, or both, I don't know.

———————

After the 2016 election results were announced, there was a movement for white people to show solidarity with BIPOC (Black, Indigenous, and people of color) by wearing a safety pin. Back home in Charlottesville, it struck me as well-intentioned but deeply stupid—a pin means nothing at all. But here, I buy a sweater (it'll become one of my favorites); the price tag is attached with a safety pin.

I put that safety pin on my lapel as a reminder to the other guests that they don't own whiteness. Or southernness, for that matter. I don't own southernness, either, but no one knows that unless I speak. Or maybe not, given the southern gentility code I can't crack. Either way, I don't because no one would actually listen if I did.

If I were to speak up—to staff, to management, to guests—any reasonable person would respond, "Well, why don't you just leave?" But it's not as if you can get a refund because "the vibe" makes your skin crawl. The only thing standing between us and the other affluent white guests—all of us patronizing the Homestead—is our belief in human rights.

And, I guess, the pin.

———

All the nostalgic grandeur at the Homestead must be in other rooms. I can't imagine any wannabe southern belle thinking this is the height of luxury. I've stayed in nicer rooms at the Hampton Inn.

Our room is at the end of a very long hallway on the main floor. By the end of our stay, my feet will ache from walking its length, at least a city block. There are 483 rooms and suites here. Ours has a king bed, two end tables, a desk chair, and a wood-composite desk that's chipped all to hell. It's alternately freezing and smothering. We asked for the fridge the room advertised—in which Brandon and I were going to store the beers we imported from Charlottesville—but it never arrived.

I know we're supposed to complain, but I also know that the people who work here will just bear the brunt of the complaints. They're probably overworked and underpaid, like most hotel employees. An Indeed. com review offers mixed reviews of employment at the Homestead under the Omni's management. The employees who seem to embrace the job are the ones doing the specialized labor—at the spa, the gun range, the bar, and the restaurant. Others—who work in the laundry, in the kitchens, in the kids' camp—speak of low wages, overwork, underwork (leading to fewer paid hours), and mold in staff housing. According to the reviews, the staff turnover is high—which is saying something in a locale with few other employment options.

During my stay, I didn't see any guests wearing MAGA hats. Even if that's where their politics lay, that's not how southern gentility rolls. But it's not that big a leap from the Homestead's celebration of its history to a desire to "make America great again." It's a nostalgia that begs the question, "Great for whom?"

Obviously not the BIPOC population and working or poor white women who've always made the best of what they were able to do—and fought for more. But it's also not the racist, working-class white men, who'd become the media's focus for the entirety of Trump's presidency. They have plenty of blame coming their way, but they wouldn't or couldn't stay at the Homestead.

It's the conservative rich. I can't guess specifically where their great times lie—what nostalgic vision they've unified around—but it's not in a world where undocumented immigrants can become citizens, where everyone has health care, where Black lives matter, and where women hold positions of power.

On our last morning there, the social climate changes. I trudge down the long hall to get my morning cup of tea and the other guests—younger and of various ethnicities—actually smile and nod at me. There are even some *good mornings*. I'm suddenly visible! I'm suddenly comfortable!

"What's the deal with people being nice all of a sudden?" I ask Brandon.

He spits out his toothpaste. "The Virginia Music Educators Association is having its conference here. I ran into my high school band director on my way to the gym."

After I shower, I'm heading out when I also see a familiar face.

"Mr. Phillip?" I ask. He looks at me and I know from his face that he has no idea who I am. "I'm one of your former students—Jennifer Niesslein? From Broad Run?"

He obviously doesn't know who I am, but in the manner of teachers everywhere, he's friendly and supportive, leaning in to return my hug.

"Broad Run! Yes! What class were you?"

He introduces me to Mrs. Phillip, and we chat for a while.

"So, what are you up to these days?"

"I'm an editor," I say. "But my son's a musician, and we're staying here because he's in the all-state jazz band."

"Good for him!" he says, and we brag about our kids—their son is also a band director—for a moment.

Looking around, he says, "It looks like a beautiful place."

"It's not my style," I say, eager to distance myself from the southern gentility, eager to assure him I did not grow up to be one of them. Lowering my voice, I add, "They nickel and dime you."

We all laugh. Later, after the concert, both of the Phillips will seek me out to congratulate me on our son's performance. I give credit to Brandon, a musician himself, and our son's own band director, whom I overhear praising our son to another teacher.

I'm suddenly yanked back into the present, among people looking toward the future, the promise of youth. I hadn't seen my child in days, and when we're finally away from his peers, I'll hug him, inhaling the fresh scent of his teenage hair.

———————

I'll wonder later if our time at the Homestead is a harbinger of things to come during Trump's presidency. What is the Homestead's nostalgic draw except as a place where human rights were abused in the name of luxury? Similarly, what is "Make America Great Again" except nostalgia for a time when many Americans didn't have the rights they do now?

Under Trump, the nation will see an acceleration of the inequality that already existed. Trump himself will accelerate it. Although his campaign targeted working-class people, particularly men, who feared their status as white people in the country slipping, his policies will largely benefit the billionaire class through the 2017 change in the tax codes and the 2020 CARES Act, in which large corporations gobble up the dollars intended for small businesses to weather the pandemic. For the most moneyed, it will be mighty nice to see this federal largesse again.

The rest of us will have to raise our voices—loudly—to remain visible: BIPOC, the LGBTQI+ community, about half of the country's white women, people with disabilities, immigrants seeking refuge, teachers, parents, and children in the nation's public schools, and everyone who just wants potable water and clean air. We'll make our visibility clear through marches and protests, action and art and soul-searching. In the political arena, we'll assert our visibility by running for elected office and voting. Democrats will take back Congress and the White House by the end of 2020, impeaching Trump twice in his single term. Yet even after all this, a good chunk of the country will still be in his thrall, this charlatan with a failed insurrection and a lost cause.

LITTLE WOMEN

The first time I saw *Little Women* on screen was in 1994—
it was the one with Winona Ryder. In the theater, my
mom, my three sisters, and I took up a good part of a row.
Before the movie started, Krissy—the third of us—said
she was going to get a drink and asked if anyone wanted
anything. We barraged her with requests. I asked last. "Do
you think they have iced tea?"

She looked at us incredulously. "I can't remember all
this shit—you guys can get your own snacks."

We watched the movie. Only Mom and I and
maybe Erin had read the book. At a critical part of the
movie, maybe when Beth is dying, Mom leaned over and
whispered to the sisters on either side of her, "*That's our
couch.*" And there it was, the sitting room couch, up on
the silver screen. They were instructed to pass it along to
the other sisters.

After the movie ended and the five of us emerged into
the cold December parking lot to pile into the car, Krissy
said, "No one told me that *I die*!"

Jill, the fourth of us, said, "Well, I'm a bratty little bitch!"

"Language," Mom said to her ten-year-old.

This is one of my favorite memories.

My mom and my sisters are my favorite women in the world. A friend in college once referred to us as the Niesslein Matriarchy, and he wasn't lying. We're that way on purpose. After the divorce, we cleaved together and became reliant on each other. Like the March sisters, we had some conflicts early on, but we've made peace and made memories and made nostalgia.

We don't have a shy, saintly Beth among us. We don't have anyone with manuscript-burning-monster tendencies. We just have our precious mouthy selves, our "Marmee" included, running to catch each other as we can.

Jill, the Amy to my Meg, emailed everyone to suggest we watch the 2019 film version of *Little Women* together, "preferably not in a theater."

"Not in the theater where I'm the server," Krissy responded.

I had already seen the movie once in a theater, with

my son, who had no idea what the plot was. I was forty-seven years old, and the last time I had seen a *Little Women* was twenty-five years ago.

Greta Gerwig's 2019 adaptation hit me hard this time. It's a good movie, possibly great, but even while I was appreciating her overtly feminist interpretation, in certain scenes I was overcome. I felt slightly out of control of my body and couldn't figure out what emotion was responsible. I held my breath because I knew that I verged on the kind of crying that crescendos into wails and decrescendos into a sobbing snot storm. This emotion peaked during the scenes with all four sisters in the same house when they're harmonious or when they're mildly bickering in that sisterly way. It peaked again when Beth dies.

Grief. The emotion was fresh grief. In the scene where Jo tries to dissuade Meg from getting married on her wedding day—which always struck me as deeply weird in other versions—Jo says, "I can't believe childhood is over." It slayed me. I can't believe my youth is over.

And if there is such a thing as a one-two punch in a two-hour-fifteen-minute movie, this was it: one of us will die first.

The summer before, my sisters and I took a vacation together with our families. On a rare occasion, just the sisters were alone together. I arrived last and Jill told me that before I got there, they were all contemplating what we would have ever done—what we would do—without our mom as an anchor. "Well, there's always Jenny," one of them said. "She'd keep us in line."

In the theater with my son, I got a little peek behind the curtain of what lies ahead. This is one reason we need personal nostalgia. Sometimes there's a good reason to avoid looking to the future. I don't know about you, but I absolutely cannot bear to open the curtain further, to imagine the scene when just three sisters are left.

Nostalgia encourages us to look to the past, all those accumulated memories that make the present so much richer. Nostalgia could care less about the future. Nostalgia knows that the future holds loss. Nostalgia tries so, so very hard to keep the curtain closed.

In the near future, I imagined then, the five of us will see the movie together. We'll be sprawled out in Mom's living room, but I'll make sure to put myself in the center. The scene where Beth dies in this newest adaptation is trickier, not as blunt as a death scene, but I'll start making noise before my own women start poking at the curtain.

I'll say, "*That's not Mom's couch.*"

DREADFUL SORRY

Pick a fight with a dead person. Lose.

—Sonya Huber
"How to Write an Essay"[2]

I watch a fair amount of reality TV about the paranormal. This is what happens when a child who devours ghost stories by Joan Lowry Nixon and Lois Duncan grows up. On some level, I know I'm being played. But I also I want to believe.

The first one that hooked me in was *Ghost Hunters*, a show about a pair of guys who used to work for Roto-Rooter and who assembled a small team to see if they could find evidence of the paranormal—or debunk the claims of locals who allege a haunting. I liked them quite a bit at first. One of the main guys—Grant—reminded me of my brother-in-law. It's not that they looked a lot alike, but they were aging the same way: circles under their eyes, a posture that spoke of some years working with their hands. The team would use various "technology" to attempt to communicate with the dead haunting the locale. My favorite part was always the EVP (electronic voice phenomena) sessions, in which a team member would ask questions into a recorder, then play it back to hear if it picked up answers they couldn't hear with their own ears. I was okay with it, for a while, when they played stuff back and it sounded to me like "whomp-whomp" and they decided the spirit was actually saying "murder." What turned me off was how they responded:

"What the . . .?!"

"Oh my God!"

"Dude!"

If I were a ghost trying to communicate with living people, I'd be highly annoyed. You're asking me to talk to you and then you freak out when I do exactly what you asked?

What's your name?

Jennifer.

OH MY GOD! DID YOU HEAR HER SAY HER NAME'S JENNIFER? CLEAR AS A BELL!

[Silently.] *For chrissakes.* [Disappears.]

Oh, I watched the similar shows—and there are many— but it was the same problem. If you want to communicate with the dead, stop the drama and communicate.

This is where the mediums come in.

TV mediums, frankly, haven't had a great run of it. When I was a preteen, daytime television introduced me to Sylvia Browne, a dour, no-BS type who herself died in 2013. I vividly remember her telling a talk show audience member that the audience member's stepfather had died by suicide on an impulse; it was brutal to watch. John Edward, a kinder, still no-BS type, was in the next cycle of TV psychics. Browne was widely debunked (she dabbled in solving missing persons cases with poor results), and I haven't seen Edward on TV in a long time.

There's a new crop in recent years. The most well-known is probably Theresa Caputo, the "Long Island Medium." She says in the intro to her show on TLC, "I like to think of myself as a typical Long Island mom." When she feels Spirit coming on to relay a message, she mashes her lips together. There's also the "Hollywood Medium," Tyler Henry, a young man who bears a striking resemblance to a younger Macaulay Culkin. His show on E! only televises his readings with celebrities. There was also Kim Russo, another medium who visited places with celebrities where they'd claimed to have paranormal or inexplicable experiences on her show, *The Haunting Of* on LMN.

My current favorite is *The Dead Files*. I like it because it features two things I love: histories of ordinary people and the paranormal. The history comes via Steve DiSchiavi, a retired NYC homicide detective. The medium is Amy Allan. She's someone my mother would call an "odd bird," which is what she says when she generally likes people but has to acknowledge they're pretty damn weird.

The Dead Files alternates segments between Amy and Steve, who don't talk to each other until the end. Amy goes on her walk through the haunted location and reports what she sees/feels/hears. The woman has seen some things. I like it best when the ghosts have actual connections to the living homeowners. Occasionally, she'll slip into something I don't especially buy, like reporting extraterrestrial beings. She generally characterizes the state of what's going down on a scale of "not good" to "really, *really* bad." Steve, on the other hand, first interviews the family affected, then reaches out to sources like local historians, genealogists, and local police chiefs to find the history of the house or land. He's the show's human factor, offering a hug or his handkerchief when his interviewee is scared or addled.

When Amy's walk is done, she meets up with a local sketch artist who then draws what she saw. The artists' talents vary widely. It's Brandon's favorite part of the show.

Okay, it's mine, too, because more often than not, it's funny. In the later seasons, there's a script. The artist asks, "Amy, is this what you saw?"

Onscreen, Amy answers, "Yes, that's what I saw."

In our own home, we say, "Yes, if a seventh-grader drew it."

Sometimes we're wrong. Viewers only see the drawing during the Reveal. Brandon and I are occasionally impressed by the better sketches that seem to square up with Steve's research. Mostly that doesn't happen. Mostly we try to find humor where we can because we're alive and middle-aged and if we're haunted, it's only by the ghosts of our dreams as younger people.

Amy talks about her walk, and Steve pipes in with some info that seems to jibe with her visions. At the end, Amy gives the affected people some advice. In the early seasons, it's generally some sage and a blessing they can administer themselves. It gets complicated later. We've seen her recommend mediums, "chaos magicians" (a vocation I'm still unclear about), Reiki masters, voodoo priests, shamans, and/or demonologists to clear the house. I've also seen her, in all seasons, recommend they move.

Brandon jokes that Amy and Steve have a real estate business on the side, buying up the haunted houses to flip them. We laugh, but part of me wants to believe in the earnestness of both Steve and Amy while another real part of me laughs for real, but there I am, every Thursday. Is it not good or really, *really* bad?

Ten years ago, I watched these shows with the same kind of interest I did as a kid; the scare factor had dissipated, but my interest in what may or may not be known was still there, more of a fascination than a yearning. I doubted that anyone I knew who died would be interested in contacting me. I wasn't primary in any dead person's life, although I held a teeny hope that the grandmother who died when I was ten would still be curious about how my life turned out.

I've written three obituaries and delivered two eulogies in the past nine years. My dead now include all my grandparents.

I miss the grandparents that I knew in adulthood, but I'm not sorry they died, if the alternative was living the way they were. The end of their lives isn't how I—or anyone—should remember them. I wasn't especially close to my paternal grandfather; apparently, he doted on me when I was a baby, but neither one of us bothered to keep connected as I grew up. But I *was* close to my maternal grandparents. I talked to them often and flew back up to Pennsylvania when they needed me. They were my friends. I long for them.

I also lost Jeff, my sister Erin's husband. Unlike my grandparents, his death was unexpected. Also unlike my grandparents, there was little love between us in the last years of his life when he lost his way. Before those years, it was still a little rocky. For decades, this is how it would go: Jeff would fuck up, I'd be mad, and he'd redeem himself in my eyes, until the next time he fucked up, I'd be mad, and he'd redeem himself in my eyes, until . . .

I do have good memories of him. The time we got kicked out of history class in high school for talking too much; his stories of dolphins jumping around his small watercraft when he went ocean kayaking on our family vacation; the relief of familiarity that hit me at our twenty-year class reunion when he sidled up and said, "Fancy seeing you here."

But even when it went south in those last years, we each deeply loved Erin and their son and we each respected that the other was important in their lives. Five years after his death, I have a hard time tasting the grief because it's mixed in a complicated frappé with anger and remorse.

We were equally headstrong with equal streaks of know-it-all-ness, but where I collected responsibility like it was my job, he dove into recklessness, again and again, in pretty much every area of his life: fast driving, motorcycling, recreational drugs, finances, the feelings of the people who were ultimately on his team. Officially, he died of a drug overdose, but he wasn't an addict. It was his recklessness that killed him.

About Jeff, I am anti-nostalgic. We all know people who've been magically transformed into saints after their deaths, but I want to remember all that he was, including his many faults—some forgivable; some not. I found some his unforgivable, chiefly that he left his body for Erin to find.

I have dreams that he just shows back up at a family gathering with no explanation for his disappearance. At first I'm elated, and that old fondness rushes back . . . and then I'm supremely pissed at the emotional carnage he's caused. In these dreams, Jeff blows me off as if I'm the one being irrational. Everyone else is thrilled to have him back, no questions asked.

I wake up and try to shake it off. Although my shows tell me that spirits will sometimes try to contact the living through dreams, I'm far more inclined to go with the regular old armchair psychologists on this one. In a family of four sisters, I'm the oldest, *Little Women*'s Meg. The responsible drudge, clucking her tongue at the people who don't play by the rules, all the while nursing a soft spot for them.

————————

When I'm watching these shows, I can't help but wonder what the mediums would tell me about my own dead. I suppose that's the whole point, to capture the hope that we're not just sacks of meat, that we have souls and that what we think of as our selves aren't just neurons in the gray matter, firing off according to our genetic and epigenetic programming. I want to believe that there's ... something to assure me that I haven't lost for an eternity the people for whom I yearn.

I daydream that my grandmothers will both come through first—I come from a long line of outspoken women. If my grandfathers come through, it'll be after them. I don't expect to hear from Jeff at all. He wouldn't give me the satisfaction. Besides, he was an atheist, a believer in what science could prove: when you die, you die, lost and gone forever. Dreadful sorry.

One evening, I put out a call to my Facebook friends for recommendations for mediums. They deliver.

I told Erin that I was writing this. That I might contact a medium to give me a reading.

"I don't believe in that. Jeff and I used to talk about how much bullshit it was," she said. "After he died, so many people told me that he got in touch with them, and I wanted to believe it for a while. But when I stepped away, I started to realize if Jeff really wanted to tell me something, he wouldn't tell it to some random person I only know because they worked at an insurance business in the same building where I worked."

"I know what you're saying. That's bizarre."

Even without the paranormal element, Erin was deluged with people—mostly former classmates Jeff hadn't seen in years—wanting to glom on to the grief. In most cases, she just blocked them on Facebook, didn't answer the door when they came knocking. At Jeff's wake, I had to kick a particularly hurtful person out, and when Erin was exhausted, I shut the whole thing down in a way that might be read as a touch aggressive.

"What kind of terrible people would take advantage of someone at the worst time in their life?" she said.

"You know . . . I sighed. "I just *want* to believe. I get you, I do. But at the same time, I think about history. I know that people used to think that bloodletting or some tonic would cure their sicknesses. But people also used to think that the earth was flat, that the sun revolved around us. So I don't know if I'm being stupid or arrogant to think that maybe someone can communicate with the dead."

"Yeah, I don't know," Erin said, and we left it at that.

———————

Stupid or arrogant? I put it out of my mind when I sign up for a thirty-minute phone session, clicking the button to transfer $200 from my PayPal account. When I get to the part of the form where I'm supposed to write who I'd like the medium to contact on my behalf, I write, "Can we just see who comes through?"

This decision might have been not good.

I wake up late on the day of my appointment, a cold February Monday. The medium had sent instructions to prep for the reading, including avoiding drinking alcohol or taking drugs during or a few hours prior. She also instructs her clients to speak to her from a place that's both physically and mentally quiet.

About an hour before my three o'clock appointment, I'm folding my laundry on my unmade bed as I talk out loud to my dead grandparents. I'm giving each of them something to mention so I know it's them. I speak to my paternal grandfather last. I'm having a hard time coming up with something because, although we loved each other in a distant way, we weren't close, for a mixed bag of reasons, including his long bout of dementia. "Grandpap," I say, floundering for a solid memory, one that wasn't told to me, "maybe say something about the time you showed us around Charleston." My husband and I had taken a vacation there over twenty years ago; Grandpap and his lovely second wife, Katie, had lived near the city then, and, like my dad does, he showed his love through hospitality.

At three, the phone rings and I push *Record* on my old-timey Radio Shack recording device.

The medium is friendly and down-to-earth. She approaches each spirit as if we're working together to figure out who they are. In a way, we are. With each spirit, she's learning more about my family constellation.

The first one is a little boy who says his name is Charlie. He says he's my mother's sister's son. He's the spirit of a child she miscarried long ago, and he delivers a reassuring message that I'll relay to my aunt later.

Next up, we have an elder who says he's my brother's father. I don't have any brothers. There's one guy I suppose is technically my stepbrother—my dad's wife has a son—

but I've never met the man, and I'm pretty sure his father is still alive. Also, he can pay for his own damn medium.

"We'll set him aside for now," the medium says.

We move on to someone whose energy is "light and fun." It's a woman in her twenties, but the medium tells me not to get caught up in the ages that she describes. "Sometimes they'll appear the age they thought they were most attractive." I laugh—call it vanity (and it is), but why *not* be hot in the afterlife? We spend a goodly amount of time with this spirit. She insists she was like a sister to me. She says she misses our "girl time." She shows the medium an array of makeup, like lipsticks. She's attracted to my energy. At one point, I say she might be my paternal grandmother, who was vivacious in the way this spirit seems to be.

"It's not your grandmother," the medium says. "Grandmothers know who they are and they announce themselves."

Finally, we get to some details. I knew her a long time ago. Her name is something like *Anna* and she died in a car accident. Ah. This describes one person I knew, although I always thought of her as an acquaintance—a friend of Erin's, back when they were in middle school. I tell the medium her name, and she says that the spirit is laughing.

"*Thank* you!" the medium says. "So simple but I couldn't hear it!"

———————

Sometimes I've stepped into the role of spokesperson for my mom and sisters. I'm good in a crisis. I don't cry easily and I can usually summon the adequate words. I'll realize later that I've come to this reading in my spokesperson role. I'll wonder if I got Erin's reading.

———————

"*Now* your grandmother's coming through," the medium says. "Oh, she's funny! She says, 'Look at you, going to a medium and not the computer!' She told me that I'll do."

Then the medium gets stuck on "Charles, Charlie, Carlton . . . ." Oh, holy hell, not this again. "Charleston."

"Wait, did you say 'Charleston'?"

"Did she live there?"

"No," I say, but I want to avoid tipping my hand. It's been like this the whole reading so far—I don't want to give the medium too much info, but I'm also mindful that my thirty minutes are ticking away and we don't have enough time to play Guess Who. At some point—possibly here—I give in to full-on collusion. "But her husband did."

Grandma reminds the medium of Liza Minnelli, either in her appearance or her larger-than-life energy. Grandma was prettier than Liza Minnelli, although I can see a passing resemblance with their large eyes and short hair. But Grandma definitely had a big personality. And that big personality has a lot of advice to give.

She wants me to take my vitamins. She wants me to ward off depression (because "the ladies" in our family tend to get depressed as they get older) by taking walks, maybe by the water. I should get my hormones in balance, and I should tell my sisters. I even get a recipe: a kind of salad with beets, garlic, parsley, apple cider vinegar, and maybe a little honey if I want to sweeten it up. The medium tells me that I can look up how those foods promote various hormones.

"What does she want me to do with her writing?" I ask. I have a manuscript of short fiction she wrote—it's funny, in a way that's of its time. And incredibly raunchy.

"She's showing me books on fire," the medium says.

"So, I'm supposed to not do anything with it? She doesn't want it out?"

The medium pauses. "*Oh*. No. Don't burn it. She wants you to publish it—do whatever, leave parts out, and write an intro about who you are. She wants it to take off like fire."

It's the deepest wish of nearly every writer I've met. I've been an editor most of my career, and part of my job is publicizing, as much as I can, each writer I've edited. Even though I know how common this desire for writerly acclaim is, I smile at my notes, sitting there in a slice of the afternoon sun. This is as close to her as I felt for years, back when she gave me *Harriet the Spy*, one voracious reader to another.

Grandpap is there with her, but he's waving his hands like *no, no, no*. He wants Grandma to do the talking. He shows himself by luxury cars, the medium says. When he was younger, she says, he was a guy-about-town. That's true—among the women he dated was my kindergarten teacher. But he doesn't have much else to say. "Sometimes the more religious elders don't like to talk to mediums."

——————

I apparently have a lot of dead waiting to talk to me. The scene in *Ghost* occurs to me—you know the one where Orlando jumps into Whoopie Goldberg's character's body to get to the front of the line of the dead waiting to communicate? *Baby, what'd you do to your hair?* After one of my spirit guides comes through—a tall blonde glamazon dressed from the thirties or forties who wants me to have more glamour in my life (not my thing in even the teeniest way)—I Orlando this situation in my own way. I ask if Jeff's there.

It's a snap decision.

———————

The medium sees a man stepping forward in a black leather motorcycle jacket with a motorcycle or motorbike. "He's handsome," she says. She pauses. "*Really* handsome . . . I'm not saying he's cocky—"

"Oh, he's cocky," I say. "He knows it."

The medium laughs and says Jeff's laughing, too.

"He says, 'Miss you. You don't have to worry about me. Come and hang out and smoke with me in the garden.'" The medium tells me that when I want to feel his presence, I could set up an altar of sorts in the garden with his picture and a candle.

This enrages me. I never spent a second worrying about Jeff after he died. I've spent years worrying about Erin and Jill, who Erin called for support when she found his body. I've spent years worrying about my nephew. Two days before the reading, Brandon and I drove up to a vineyard to see him play a show. He sang an original about growing up that slayed me. Wine-tipsy, I hustled to the women's room where I tried to fix my tear-smudged mascara with rough paper towels and, although there was someone peeing in a stall, I repeated out loud to myself, "Get it together. Pull your shit together." I couldn't go back out there all weepy in front of my nephew.

Through the medium, Jeff says he visits me in my dreams, but I don't get it.

"I'm mad at him," I tell the medium.

"'Why?' he says." The medium adds, "He knows why."

I don't say anything. In this moment, I 100 percent believe I'm talking to Jeff, and it'll only occur to me later that I'm paying money to give him the silent treatment.

"Well, I'm dead," Jeff says through the medium.

He apologizes over and over. He says that he's tired. He says that he lied. He's sorry, he's sorry, he's sorry. But he feels better. He thinks he might have been bipolar or something.

The medium says that he had a really rough childhood, and that was the demon he couldn't outrun. She describes someone punching him in the jaw. She emphasizes how terrible his childhood was. I'll research later and find that the *Washington Post* published an extensive investigation that his family's church was more like a cult, with child abuse—including sexual—running rampant.

But at this moment, I'm hard. "What does he want me to tell his family?"

He goes into a litany of *I'm sorry* and *I lied* again. "In his mind, he thinks they're better off without him," the medium says. "There might be a big loss, but there's also peace."

This isn't true.

The medium tells me that he's handing out roses: a white one to her, to thank her for the reading, and a white one to me, and white and yellow ones with baby's breath for Erin.

We're over my time and she has another client waiting for a phone call. "Is there anyone else?" she asks.

"Tell Gram and Pap I love them," I say.

They tell me that they love me and they're with me. There's some more talk of getting hormones in balance, then Gram says that she'll try to visit me in my dreams, and Pap blows me a kiss.

At the end of each episode of *The Dead Files*, production gives an update on whether the haunted living people followed Amy's advice. If they did, the activity generally stops or decreases. If they didn't, the activity continues. That's what they say, anyway, a handy loop of self-validation.

I knew what *The Dead Files* clients were thinking when they agreed to do whatever Amy instructed. Right afterward, I was a true believer, although I knew even at the time that my skepticism would kick in at some point. I can understand why, a few days out, a homeowner would think, "Wait—why am I looking for a chaos magician again?"

Right after the reading, I was on an adrenaline high. Years ago, I would have called Gram and Pap—my only friends who were home during the day—but now that Mom is retired, I call her and relay what happened. I tell my sister Krissy and Dad. I debate whether to tell Erin and Jill because I don't want to retraumatize them, but news travels fast with the Niessleins, and Erin and Jill want to talk to me.

When I call, Jill's tied up and I talk to Erin a little before I tell the whole story to both of them. "Did you talk to Jeff?" she asks.

I say that I did. I tell her about his "Well, I'm dead" remark—like, what the hell is he supposed to do about it now?

"Smart-ass," she says, with a small huff of a laugh.

Later, when I recount the whole reading to Erin and Jill on speakerphone, Jill's on board, but Erin seems annoyed. "It's too vague," she says. "And Jeff knows I hate roses."

Inevitably, my skepticism kicked in. I relistened to the tapes and heard when my voice changed from its professional register, bright and high, to its natural register, lower and more contemplative. (I hear, though, how it could be read as depressive—no wonder I got so much advice about vitamins and walks by the water and glamming myself up.) I heard when I started spitting information to the medium.

I led her to most of what she told me. I wound up with Erin's middle school friend by the process of elimination. I'm the one who asked about Grandma's writing. I asked for Jeff and eventually told her he was my brother-in-law.

Other bits were way off. The elderly gent looking for my nonexistent brother. The recurrence of Charlie—the only Charlie I knew was my nephew's late, great guinea pig. And Jeff handing out roses, a flower that Erin famously dislikes.

And yet. There was the way that Grandma called my sisters and me "the ladies" (a phrase her daughter uses) and Gram called us "the girls," which is what we call ourselves and what everyone in the family calls us. Jeff's telling me to hang out in the garden—which is Erin's passion. And the alleged words of a confirmed smart-ass that helped me the most.

To this day, I still don't know if I'm being arrogant or stupid. Probably stupid or at least too vulnerable.

But for five years, I'd been fighting with Jeff, entirely in my head. After my reading, I don't. I'm not looking for another reading, but ultimately I cherish this one. I paid $200 to a stranger who helped me develop some empathy for Jeff and his struggles and who made me realize our little dynamic is over, no take-backs and no redeeming himself to me, because, well, he's dead.

MIGHTY WHITE OF ME

I'm in my maternal grandparents' yard, deep in the country darkness, fresh from a bath with my two sisters, our wet hair brushed away from our faces. Over our underpants, we all wear Pap's cotton T-shirts, cool against our skin in the western Pennsylvania summer air.

I run barefoot through the plush northern grass, trying to catch the lightning bugs. I'm a little older now, eight or nine, and soon I stop running. I think I've figured out the trick: plant yourself where the flickering is thickest and don't smoosh them in your hands. We'll enlist one of the adults to help us make a home for the lightning bugs—a glass jar that once used to hold jelly or mayo, knife holes puncturing the metal lid. Whichever one of us sisters who doesn't have a bug in hand is dispatched to create the habitat: handfuls of grass, leaves. The habitat is an afterthought, something a kind adult will dump out after we nod off on Gram and Pap's living room floor in a pile of quilts and pillows.

But in the moment, in the yard, we capture ordinary magic in our hands.

———————

In my memory, ordinary magic filled my childhood. I had a chemistry set in our cellar where I could combine ingredients to smell like lilacs. When we got a three-foot aboveground pool, my sisters and I figured out that if we ran around the edges enough, we could develop a whirlpool situation and float, pampered, on top of the swirling waters. I learned to read and read so much, so voraciously, I wanted to become someone who could create that magic for other people.

I remember so many details about my childhood that sometimes it freaks out my family of origin. The puckery taste of raw rhubarb from our rhubarb patch. The specific hue of blue on my sisters' lips when we stayed in the pool too long. The nights when the carnival came to town, Erin and I in our bunk beds, our windows open to let in the breeze and the smell of fresh-cut grass, and beyond that a carnival barker imploring over a loudspeaker, "Come see the half-lady, half-baby!"

But I can't remember what didn't exist.

I didn't know any Black people until I was ten years old.

Nearly everyone I know questions me on this. No classmates? No teachers? No one at church? Nope, nope, nope.

New Galilee was all white. I'm certain that's not the reason we moved there. Dad went to an all-white Catholic elementary school—there weren't Black Catholics in the area, he says—and he only knew a handful of Black kids at his public high school. But Mom grew up in an integrated town. In her elementary school pictures, she's always in the top row, a tall white girl among tall Black boys and girls, the Greek Americans and Italian Americans rows down. By the time my parents had us, though, they just wanted somewhere affordable, and with the birth of their third daughter, we'd grown out of our rental in Baden. All-white places like this exist all over the country.

I don't remember a single conversation about race at home. Not even on the cusp of starting fifth grade at Beaver Falls Middle School, where I'd surely meet Black students and teachers. "We wanted you girls to treat people like you'd like to be treated," Mom said when I asked her recently. For our whole lives, my sisters and I knew that we couldn't make fun of anything about a person they couldn't help. If we made fun of, say, someone's appearance, Mom, ever the special-ed teacher, would say, "Nope. If you don't like someone, you need a better reason than what they look like." She wanted us to be kind—confident enough to be kind—and race fit into that category. "Talking to you about Black people wasn't a thing," she said. It's not as if white parents were expected to have a You-Are-Going-to-Meet-a-Black-Person talk with their kids.

At the same time, I know that I'd heard the N-word before I ever met a Black person because I can't remember ever asking anyone what the word meant. But then something weird happens with my uncanny memory: a wall goes up. I can hear Pap asking someone to pass the "Dago bread" and mentioning "colored people." The N-word was acceptable in my extended family, although I was forbidden to use it. I was raised to be a respectable girl, as were all the girls in my family. (*Boys . . . well, what could you do?*) I'm sure relatives—men I loved—used the N-word, but I can't recall the memory; I can't hear it in their voices. It's not a conscious choice. It's a protective reflex to safeguard my nostalgia, my innocence. It's a kind of white mental contortionism that my brain performs to make me believe myself unscathed by white supremacy.

———

In September 2019, the City of Pittsburgh's Office of Inequity released the results of its study on race and gender in an effort to better understand how gender and race affect the lives of its citizens.[3] The study looked at the stats among different demographics and compared them to the same demographics of cities of similar sizes and makeup. The data show Black people in Pittsburgh can expect worse life outcomes compared to Black residents of other American cities at nearly every turn. Black men's quality of life was found to be terrible, but Black women fare even worse by metrics including income, employment, health, educational opportunities, birth defect rates, life expectancy, and more.

One of the study's authors, Junia Howell, an assistant professor of sociology at the University of Pittsburgh, told the news outlet *Public Source*: "What this means is that if Black residents got up today and left and moved to the majority of any other cities in the U.S., automatically by just moving their life expectancy would go up, their income would go up, their educational opportunities for their children would go up as well as their employment."

If it's this unjust now, I can't even imagine what it must have been like forty years ago. What does it mean to feel such strong nostalgia for a region that's demonstrably bad for a particular demographic—in this case, Black women?

3 https://apps.pittsburghpa.gov/redtail/images/7109_Pittsburgh%27s_Inequality_Across_Gender_and_Race_09_18_19.pdf

———————

Although I've only ever been to Pittsburgh proper a handful of times, my nostalgia for the region is strong. Driving to my cousin's wedding in 2012, we were barely past the Maryland border before my accent changed. "How far away are we from the hahse?" I asked my husband, Brandon. He glanced over at me, but he was used to this—I unknowingly slip into the accent at the slightest push. A 2014 poll conducted by Gawker Media found the (mostly white) Pittsburgh accent the "ugliest" in the nation, but to me it sounds like home, like family, like comfort.

Even the *look* of white people in Pittsburgh comforts me. As an adult, I flew into the Pittsburgh airport, sometimes to visit, once when Pap was undergoing an emergency carotid artery surgery, another time to help Gram after her double knee-replacement surgery. Many of the employees at the airport looked like they could be related to me, a certain combo of ethnicities—those whose ancestors weren't "good" white—particular to the region: Dad's puppy dog eyes, Gram's thin lips, my own sturdy hips.

And, holy hell, the food speaks to me. The best of it comes from the ethnic clubs that dot the Rust Belt, clubs that just don't exist where I live: pierogis, stuffed cabbage rolls, spaghetti dinners made with sauce recipes from Italian American ancestors, not culinary school. When Gram died in 2017, my mom, sisters, and I were at her house in Muse, picking out an outfit for her to be buried in. It was a Friday, fish fry day. I asked Brandon to go to the Muse Italian Club, as Pap had done for so many years, for the best fish sandwiches I've ever tasted and ever will. We ate that comfort back in the hotel lobby. No one acknowledged this would be the last time.

To me, Pittsburgh is an emblem for my childhood, my ancestry, a way of understanding how my foremothers shaped who I'd become. Pittsburgh stands in for all of western Pennsylvania, where I was raised.

Reading about Pittsburgh's treatment of Black men and women surprised me. I knew it wasn't a racial utopia by a long shot, but the absolute worst in the country? In Pittsburghese, there's a specific word to shut down isms: "ignerant." (You can pronounce it with two syllables or three.) It means being willfully stupid or offensive. I always took it to mean pretending not to know better. In that way, it's the opposite of "ignorant," which implies a kind of innocence. So if a person says something offensive about a category of other humans, you could tell them,

"You're being ignorant." It's the perfect rebuke to racist comments. I never corrected a racist adult this way because I was a child. And while I might have lobbed it at another child when they made fun of the fat kid or the kid who always smelled, I never corrected another child about race. Because before fifth grade, it was just not a factor in my daily life.

———————

A few years ago, I published an essay by Amy E. Robillard, a writer and a professor of English and rhetoric at Illinois State University, at my online magazine, *Full Grown People*. She wrote:

> When I teach undergraduates about the concept of ideology, I ask them to think about it using the metaphor of marinade. As products of an ideology, we are the meat that is being marinated. The marinade is the ideology—the coherent set of values, beliefs, and ideals that guides our thoughts and actions, that shapes our perception of reality, and that largely remains invisible. When a piece of meat has marinated in a mixture of seasonings and sauce for a long time, the marinade becomes part

of the meat. It infuses and is therefore inseparable from the meat. One can no more easily remove the marinade from the meat than one can remove the brain from the body. And a piece of meat needs time to marinate. One cannot marinate a piece of meat in five minutes, just as one cannot subscribe to a new ideology in a week.[4]

In retrospect, I've been marinating in whiteness most of my life. Whiteness only exists in the context of what privilege white people have relative to people of other races, as they're defined now. But racism wouldn't exist without whiteness. In fact, the true name of racism is white supremacy.

———————

Anyone raising kids can tell you, fifth grade is usually when kids start to publicly distance themselves from their grown-ups. When my son was in fifth grade, the school invited parents to the pre-Thanksgiving lunch. The kids fled to the other side of the cafeteria. "Are all of them trying to pretend they have their own condos somewhere now?" I asked Brandon on the way out.

4 Amy E. Robillard, "Knee Jerk," *Full Grown People*, June 1, 2017. http://fullgrownpeople.com/2017/06/01/knee-jerk/

The summer before my own fifth grade, I wasn't much different. One evening, my sisters and I were hanging out at the top of the steps that led down to Locust Avenue. A rising sixth-grader, smoking a cigarette, was walking by on the street below. For reasons unknown, five-year-old Krissy hollered down, "Fathead!"

"What did you call me?" she called up to us.

"A fathead!" Krissy yelled.

"*Stop it*," I hissed at Krissy. The last thing I needed was negative attention from an eleven-year-old who smoked.

I worried about a lot of things. Navigating the multistory building. Being in a city. Going to school with a lot of kids—eighth-graders—who looked like adults to me. Getting beat up by a "fathead." And meeting so many kids from other elementary schools, some of them Black.

I grew up watching *Sesame Street* and *The Electric Company* and, later *The Jeffersons*, *Good Times*, and *What's Happening!!* The shows taught me that Black people live in cities. The local TV news taught me that Black people perpetrated violent crimes in the city, although I knew I had a least one relative I was never allowed to meet because he was a violent criminal. Beyond that, I had no context.

As it turned out, of course, meeting Black kids was no big deal. The switch-up in racial demographics was slightly disorienting, but even that lasted just a week before it became the new normal. Black children made up about a third of our class. Throughout the school year, I made a handful of new Black friends, a handful of new white friends.

My homeroom and social studies teacher was Mrs. Paulette Potter. I adored her. In researching this, I discovered Mrs. Potter was a civil rights icon: a Black woman who grew up in Beaver County, she developed and taught the first Black history course at Beaver Falls High School—back in 1971. As a 2005 *Pittsburgh Post-Gazette* article put it, "Before she taught history, she made it—becoming the first instructor at the school to teach such a course." It was unusual for both the time and place. This was just a few years after the Jim Crow era supposedly ended. I didn't even know how lucky I was to have her as a teacher.

———

In hindsight, I don't feel especially bad about my nostalgia for my western Pennsylvania childhood. We all have to grow up somewhere, and there is no place in the United States that isn't problematic in one way or another. Everyone deserves to sink into the pockets of joy in their memories, no matter their race.

When the steel industry tanked, taking Dad's job with it, we moved to Sterling, Virginia, an exurb of Washington, DC I was and still am riddled with nostalgia—I deeply missed our house in New Galilee, and I've had silly fantasies about buying it back.

In my Sterling middle school, I didn't learn a whole lot about race. Seneca Ridge Middle School was whiter than Beaver Falls, but not as white as New Galilee. I do have an artifact from seventh grade social studies, which is essentially a one-girl slam book about Ronald Reagan. His political ascendance was terrible for all financially unstable Americans. It wasn't until later in high school, when we got past all the dead white male canon, that all of us in Honors English got to read contemporary writers. This was the writing that wedged open the door between what I wanted to do and what actual people were doing. Alice Walker made a huge impression on me; I sought out her books at the library and dreamed about someday naming a daughter after a character in her novel *The Temple of My Familiar*.

In college, I took a good amount of women's studies and African American studies courses. Intellectually, I learned a lot about the injustices our country imposed on whoever wasn't white. But socially I doubted anyone outside my race would want to befriend me. The more

I learned about whiteness, the more tentative I became about bringing it up. Why would any Black person trust me enough for us to get to know each other? There's a certain truth there, but it also plays in to how white supremacy was set up in the first place: to keep white people apart from and above those of any other race or identity, especially Black.

White supremacy has given me and other white people some good shit. We aren't assumed to have a monolithic culture as other races unfairly are. In my family of origin, we have many of the demographic markers Black Americans are stereotyped for having. Two of my three sisters were teenage mothers. Some of their partners served time. One died of a drug overdose. We've been on food stamps. And yet we're middle-class white people with all the bonuses that come with whiteness. No one has ever followed me around in a store. I've never had trouble getting a loan. I've never feared for my life based on the color of my skin.

However, white supremacy exacts a price. We get public service announcements that don't just aim to prevent teen pregnancy, but go that extra mile to demonize teenage mothers. We get policies recommending jail time for nonviolent crimes. We get different reactions to drug addiction: scorn for Black addicts, sympathy for white ones. We get shamed for needing public assistance, although both Black and white citizens tend to be on it for a short time—unlike multimillion-dollar corporations, headed by white boards and CEOs who receive far more benefits than any struggling family.

―――――――

I've spent too many years of my life pretending that I wasn't indifferent to white supremacy. I'd pop up like Punxsutawney Jen whenever racial injustice made the news, briefly vocal about it. I know a younger version of myself would say I wasn't indifferent, just busy with my own life. It was true. I had a little kid to raise, work to achieve, a marriage to maintain, extended family crises and celebrations to attend. But the same must be said for, say, the Black women in Pittsburgh.

I can pinpoint the first time I viscerally felt my own white supremacy.

When my son, Caleb, was sixteen, he got his driver's license, and on his first solo trip, to a music lesson, his car gave up the ghost on an on-ramp. He called me, unsure what to do. I tried to quash my panic, imagining the traffic on 250 whizzing by my baby just yards away. "Oh, hang on," he said. "A police officer is here."

I was flooded with relief. A minute later, I realized this is what white supremacy looks like: I can feel relieved that a cop is there to help my white son while any parent of a Black child would be terrified.

———————

I can't pinpoint when I realized I'd been played—it was more of a gradual dawning. But at some point, I recognized that my own white complacency opened a void into which the dormant mobs of active, violent white supremacists could enter and claim whiteness for themselves. It was happening for years—on the dark web, on the regular internet, in real-time meetings—before it came to my town.

I live in Charlottesville, Virginia, and in August 2017, the Unite the Right rally brought all stripes of fringe white supremacists to our city to occupy a park where a statue of Robert E. Lee is placed (it was removed in 2021). The city council had voted to remove it but was blocked by the Virginia government. A local man organized the rally. Like me, he'd graduated from the University of Virginia, marinating in the idea he was special just by virtue of attending the school. From what I understand, after graduation, he lived a normal, albeit unremarkable life, even left-leaning for a time. Charlottesville is the kind of city where it's hard to stand out because whatever your field is, someone else here already has a genius grant for the same thing. This man found his way to stand out by attacking a Black city councilor on Twitter in 2016. He found further specialness by bringing explicit hate to Charlottesville.

On Friday, August 11, 2017, white men with tiki torches marched through my alma mater, chanting, "You will not replace us," which morphed into "Jews will not replace us."

I was blasé at first, only hearing "You will not replace us." I thought of the site of the Unite the Right protest, Lee Park (later called Emancipation Park, now called Market Street Park), and the homeless folks who hang out there in nice weather. Dudes, I thought, you will definitely be replaced on Sunday when your little shit show is over.

I didn't go to the counterprotest for health reasons—one whiff of tear gas and I'd be dead of asthma—but I watched from afar with increasing horror. The invading white supremacists shot guns at a Black man's feet, severely beat a Black man in a parking garage next to the police station, killed a white woman, and traumatized our citizens physically and emotionally. When the white supremacists were finally ordered to disperse, I watched a contingent of them, from my back porch, walk to the park where my son used to play Little League.

The next weekend, we took Caleb to college for the first time. After getting him settled in his dorm, Brandon and I went back to the hotel. We sat at the nondescript bar, having a beer or two. At some point, four white men in polo shirts and khakis entered the bar and stood behind us, watching whatever was on TV and enjoying their drinks. My body went on high alert. I didn't feel safe with them standing behind me. They looked too much like the men bearing tiki torches. I had to get out of there.

———————

I'm writing this as Americans across the country are protesting police killings of Black and Brown men, women, and children for no reason. Whites have brutalized Blacks on this land since 1619, even before there was such a thing as the United States of America, but this latest wave of protest brings the slaughter to horrifying life with the technology of cell phone cameras. A 2020 *Washington Post* five-year study found that, on average, police officers kill about a thousand citizens a year, a full 50 percent of them Black, although the population of Black citizens is only about 18 percent nationwide. (This doesn't even count citizens killed while in custody or those, like Trayvon Martin or Ahmaud Arbery, killed by white supremacist vigilantes.)

NPR compiled a noncomprehensive list[5] of some of the victims and what they were doing right before their murders:

Eric Garner had just broken up a fight, according to witness testimony.

Ezell Ford was walking in his neighborhood.

Michelle Cusseaux was changing the lock on her home's door when police arrived to take her to a mental health facility.

Tanisha Anderson was having a bad mental health episode, and her brother called 911.

Tamir Rice was playing in a park.

Natasha McKenna was having a schizophrenic episode when she was tazed in Fairfax, Virginia.

Walter Scott was going to an auto parts store.

Bettie Jones answered the door to let Chicago police officers in to help her upstairs neighbor, who had called 911 to resolve a domestic dispute.

Philando Castile was driving home from dinner

5 https://www.npr.org/2020/05/29/865261916/a-decade-of-watching-black-people-die

with his girlfriend.

Botham Jean was eating ice cream in his living room in Dallas.

Atatiana Jefferson was babysitting her nephew at home in Fort Worth, Texas.

Eric Reason was pulling into a parking spot at a local chicken and fish shop.

Dominique Clayton was sleeping in her bed.

Breonna Taylor was also asleep in her bed.

And George Floyd was at the grocery store.

By now, the list is out of date. And no matter who I add—like Antwon Rose, a teenager in Pittsburgh—it'll still be out of date by the time you read this. That's how often Black people die at the hands of the police. To date, no law enforcement officers have been held accountable for the murders committed. White supremacy is part of two major US institutions: police training and the judiciary.

But frankly, it's in every institution.

Years ago, I decided I needed to push back against my complicity in a racist system. It's not good for anyone of any race. I think about the Christians in Germany during the rise of the Nazi Germany, going about their daily lives, keeping silent, assuming other people would take care of the growing danger.

I don't know if we're on the verge of a weird civil war or not, a war not divided by geography but ideology. We certainly have the body count to qualify. It feels like it to me, but maybe it's just because I'm relatively new to the work. But I've also never felt our country slipping into authoritarianism as I feel it is right now.

When I search for what I can give to a democratic fight against white supremacy, I have a few things in my arsenal. Money, power, and outreach to my elected officials. I spend the most money for local causes because a lot of white supremacy happens on a local level. My job as an editor gives me power to elevate Black voices. I write letters to my representatives and I know what's up in my local, state, and federal governments. You probably have other powers in your skill set. White people: it's time to release that ordinary magic in your hands.

So what do I do with my nostalgia? By definition, nostalgia is backward-looking, a golden-lit memory of the past.

I'm a true nostalgic, but I'm also someone who wants progressiveness, dignity, equality, equity. I feel that deeply inside myself. It's a tricky thing to square.

This summer, I talked to Caleb about it. He's an adult now, twenty-one, and any nostalgia I feel about him as a baby or kid is overshadowed by the wonderful man he's become. "But isn't part of nostalgia for a place," he said, "meaning you love it enough to make it better?"

No, not according to the old definitions forged by Europeans and Russians, the mopey yearning for a place and time that's gone, baby, gone.

But yes, in a way. We can't change the definition of nostalgia, but we don't have to react to it with pining and sorrow. We can look at it as a form of love and respond with the knowledge that at right this minute, we're creating the nostalgia for future generations. Injecting some hope into nostalgia? It's the most American thing I've ever heard anyone say.

ACKNOWLEDGEMENTS

Thanks to the wonderful team at Belt Publishing, especially to my editor, Martha Bayne, whose work made this book so much stronger, and publisher Anne Trubek, whose newsletter made me want to work with Belt in the first place.

Thank you to Ryan Schnurr, who first published "New Galilee" at *Belt Magazine* and to Brad Listi, who first published "So Happy Together" at the *Nervous Breakdown*.

So much gratitude to all the lovelies who lent me their expertise and/or perspective: Tony Esoldo, Beth Fuller, Laurel Reiman Henneman, Nicole Logorda, Valerie Sweeney, and Andrea Walter.

I'm immensely thankful to my fellow writers who gave me feedback, cheered me on, and kept me accountable. My fabulous writing group (at various times): Nell Boeschenstein, Lisa Cooper Ellison, Mary Esselman, Sharon Harrigan, and especially Jane Friedman. My dear Stephanie Wilkinson, who's still my ideal reader. And my friends and sensitivity editors, Denne Michele Norris and Deesha Philyaw. I know what a gift your work on this book is, and I don't take it for granted. Also, anything cringeworthy in this book is on me.

I know how lucky I am to have the sort of past I can look back on with joy. My family of origin—Mom, Erin, Krissy, Jill, and Dad—created that life for me. I couldn't have written this without you.

And to Brandon and Caleb, my love and my heart, thank you for everything.